P9-CFF-510

PENGUIN CANADA

WHEN ALL YOU HAVE IS HOPE

FRANK O'DEA is an entrepreneur who was a founding partner of the Second Cup coffee chain and several other successful businesses. He is a sought-after public speaker, and lives in Ottawa with his wife and two daughters.

WHEN ALL
YOU HAVE IS HOPE

[Frank O'Dea]

with John Lawrence Reynolds

PENGUIN
CANADA

PENGUIN CANADA

Published by the Penguin Group

Penguin Group (Canada), 90 Eglinton Avenue East, Suite 700,
Toronto, Ontario, Canada M4P 2Y3 (a division of Pearson Canada Inc.)

Penguin Group (USA) Inc., 375 Hudson Street, New York, New York 10014, U.S.A.
Penguin Books Ltd, 80 Strand, London WC2R 0RL, England
Penguin Ireland, 25 St Stephen's Green, Dublin 2, Ireland (a division of Penguin Books Ltd)
Penguin Group (Australia), 250 Camberwell Road, Camberwell, Victoria 3124, Australia
(a division of Pearson Australia Group Pty Ltd)
Penguin Books India Pvt Ltd, 11 Community Centre, Panchsheel Park,
New Delhi – 110 017, India
Penguin Group (NZ), 67 Apollo Drive, Rosedale, North Shore 0632, New Zealand
(a division of Pearson New Zealand Ltd)
Penguin Books (South Africa) (Pty) Ltd, 24 Sturdee Avenue, Rosebank,
Johannesburg 2196, South Africa

Penguin Books Ltd, Registered Offices: 80 Strand, London WC2R 0RL, England

First published in a Viking Canada hardcover by Penguin Group (Canada),
a division of Pearson Canada Inc., 2007
Published in this edition, 2008

5 6 7 8 9 10 (WEB)

Copyright © Frank O'Dea, 2007

Author representation: Westwood Creative Artists
94 Harbord Street, Toronto, Ontario M5S 1G6

All rights reserved. Without limiting the rights under copyright reserved above, no part of this
publication may be reproduced, stored in or introduced into a retrieval system, or transmitted
in any form or by any means (electronic, mechanical, photocopying, recording or otherwise),
without the prior written permission of both the copyright owner and the above publisher of
this book.

Manufactured in Canada.

Library and Archives Canada Cataloguing in Publication data available
upon request to the publisher.

ISBN 978-0-14-305255-5

Except in the United States of America, this book is sold subject to the condition that it shall
not, by way of trade or otherwise, be lent, re-sold, hired out, or otherwise circulated without
the publisher's prior consent in any form of binding or cover other than that in which it is
published and without a similar condition including this condition being imposed on the
subsequent purchaser.

Visit the Penguin Group (Canada) website at **www.penguin.ca**

Special and corporate bulk purchase rates available; please see
www.penguin.ca/corporatesales or call 1-800-810-3104, ext. 2477 or 2474

To my wife, Nancy, without whose love and support recovery would have been a far more difficult challenge.
To Taylor and Morgan, two of the best girls a dad could ever wish for.
To my brother Sean and sister-in-law Michèle, whose integrity, unfailing loyalty, and good judgment I can always count on.
To my brother Bill and sister, Maureen, who were and are there for me, more than they know.

No, I'll not, Carrion Comfort, despair,
Not feast on thee;
Not untwist—slack they may be—these last strands of man
In me or, most weary, cry I can no more! *I can;*
Can something—hope, wish day come, not choose not to be.

—GERARD MANLEY HOPKINS

WHEN ALL
YOU HAVE IS HOPE

ONE

It Should Have Been Happy and Warm

I stumble against the doorway. Must have drifted off there for a moment. Almost dropped the precious coins I'm holding.

I open my hand to count the money. Twenty-five … thirty-five … I lose track and start over again. Fifty. Fifty-five. Sixty-five. Seventy-five cents.

It is just after three o'clock. I am twenty-five cents short.

The wind comes up, carrying the rain with it. Cold December rain that is certain to become snow by evening. Bad news. The lineup at the Salvation Army hostel will be longer than usual this evening.

I need that twenty-five cents, that quarter of a dollar. I need it in a way I need air. I need it more than food.

I need to use the bathroom, too. Cold air does that to you. But first I need to drink. Everything is needs. I am beyond wants.

If I stand deeper in the doorway, the dirt-crusted windowed doorway of this empty store on Jarvis Street, I'll be out of the wind a little and won't shiver quite so violently. There won't be as much chilling breeze to pull at the T-shirt and plaid flannel work shirt that I have been wearing for ... for weeks now. I tried to figure out how many weeks it's been just then. Lost count.

That's not true. I did not lose count. I just don't want to know.

Standing here deeper in the doorway, I'm not seen so easily by people going by, and if I'm not seen, I can't make eye contact with somebody who might give me a quarter.

Like this fellow coming up the street. Wearing a coat with a fur collar. Smiling to himself as though somebody told him a joke, or he just decided what to buy his girlfriend for Christmas.

He looks my age. Twenty-three, twenty-four years old. Nice shoes. Good haircut. What's twenty-five cents to him? I step out into the wind again, my hand extended.

Damn.

A police car just turned the corner at Shuter Street. Coming this way. I know the cop driving it. A mean SOB. Big guy. Thick black moustache. He'll stop at the curb, tell me to get the hell off the street. Maybe he'll get out of the car and slap the money from my hand, knock the coins into the gutter and stand there watching me shuffle away, down the street and around the corner. I couldn't take that. Not today. I withdraw my hand, step back into the doorway.

I need to take the chance.

"Any spare change?" I ask the man with the fur collar as he passes me.

I startled him. He averts his eyes from mine, dropping them to my dirty plaid shirt, stained trousers, worn shoes, then away again.

Maybe he smells me. I know I smell. I can't help it. You get sick, you don't wash often enough, you don't change your clothes, that's what happens. You smell. I want to explain this to him, but he keeps walking, not missing a stride.

The police car passes. The officer hasn't noticed me either.

Three hours to beg twenty-five cents here on the street. If I get seventy-five cents, a dollar for the wine and fifty cents for the flop-house, I won't have to go to the hostel tonight. I can share a room with Bruce and Doc and the other guys.

The rain is getting heavier, the sky greyer, the air colder.

Here comes a woman, older than me, with a sweet face. I'll smile at her, maybe remind her of her own son or a long-lost brother. Women are more generous than men.

I force a smile to my face. It almost hurts. When did it start hurting to smile?

That was me, the guy looking for a handout, begging money for a bottle of wine and a fifty-cent bed in a flophouse.

The year was 1971. I was thirty years away from being named an Officer of the Order of Canada, twenty years away from marrying a beautiful and successful woman and fathering our two precious daughters, ten years away from earning my first million dollars, and a week away from deciding that I must either change or die.

LET ME PAINT YOU a pleasant picture, one you may envy.

It's the 1950s, the golden era of the nuclear family. One of the most popular shows on television is *Father Knows Best*. Father, as portrayed on the show, is a pleasant fellow who smiles easily and is a fount of common sense to his children. He holds an executive position and earns an impressive salary. We know this because he wears a well-tailored suit; lives in a large, immaculate house; drives a new car; and is married to a woman who adores him.

His wife always wears an apron and sensible shoes. She stays home to "keep house." Father is handsome, mother is pretty, and the children are attractive. The house is located in a comfortable upscale community, far from the dirt and dangers of inner-city life. The yard has a garden. The family owns a dog. The pantry is always full. The rooms are always warm. Sundays are for church. Summers are spent at a cottage on a lake. Christmas is a joyous time.

This is not only the setting for a corny sitcom. It was the setting of my life as a child, the second of four children, and it appears as idyllic on the surface as the television program it seems to mimic.

Father Knows Best existed on a Hollywood set. At 116 Ballantyne Avenue, in the community of Montréal-Ouest during the 1950s, the picture may have been similarly attractive, but the reality was not.

My father was a good man, intelligent and hard-working, the manager of a paint factory. You would have liked him if you met him. Tall, slim, and dark-haired, he was a handsome guy who carried himself with the grace and balance of a professional athlete, which he was for a time. He had an Irish aspect to his personality that many people found attractive, namely a talent for connecting both with blue-collar guys working in a tool shop and with stiff-necked politicians sitting on one of the community service boards to which he had volunteered his time.

This was a good man, in so many ways. Despite what happened, of the one time in my life that he failed me in the way that a father should never fail his son, I loved him and I know he loved me. We just had difficulty showing it.

Dad believed that everybody should meet his or her obligations. He also believed in the demonstrated superiority of English-speaking people. This did not seem nearly as alien then as it does today—most Anglos of his generation felt the same way. He had, I know, great affection and admiration for the Québécois people he lived among, including my mother, whose French-Canadian roots were as deep as anyone's. But at the core of his soul, I know that he thought Anglos superior, just as white people in the U.S. South thought themselves superior to Afro-Americans a few generations ago, though my father displayed none of that bitterness.

My father did not believe in excessive displays of emotion. I think his reaction, if he observed the way I openly hug and kiss my wife and children today, would be somewhere between embarrassment and amusement. He never expressed his opinions to us, his children, or asked about our views on anything of substance. A gulf existed between us that neither was able to bridge. We never exchanged ideas or opinions because only one opinion counted: his. This wasn't simple arrogance on his part; just a basic belief that the role of parents was to pass on knowledge to their children, a flow that was always one way. It's an old-fashioned idea, and a respectable one by some measures.

Dad never played games with us, nor did he participate in sports, a curious decision since he had been a gifted athlete in his youth, playing on the varsity football team for the University of

Manitoba. He was even asked to join the Winnipeg Blue Bombers organization and might have launched a career in the Canadian Football League if he hadn't suffered a serious knee injury.

He did not encourage me to play hockey as a child; I made that decision on my own. When I suffered a mild concussion in one game, I was banished from participating in any organized sport from that day forward, as were my brothers and sister.

Dad told us what was good and what was not good about the world. He revealed his expectations of himself, and the expectations he had of his family. Everything else between us was either not worth discussing or superfluous. He provided the means for food and shelter, moral guidance, wise counsel at his discretion, and gentle discipline when needed. We, his children, were not to expect anything more. Today he would be called a distant parent. Back then, he was simply our father.

My mother adored my father. Sixty-odd years ago, this was more than a mere romantic notion. Her kind of adoration meant that she functioned quite happily in her husband's shadow. While he was alive, my mother concealed her own strengths and much of her personality, never wanting to compete with Dad's role. Only after his death did she and her children discover just how formidable those strengths were, and then for a tragically short time.

They were an ideal fit, my father and mother. Even as a small boy, I realized how beautiful my mother was, and how she strived to make herself attractive for my father. She did this, I understand now, not only because she truly loved my father but because she was grateful and honoured to be his wife. This was based in part on practical and cultural factors. He was a white-collar anglophone. She was a middle-class Québécoise. In today's terms, my father was a catch, the Perfect Husband for a French-speaking girl, and my mother never forgot it.

Mother shared his belief in the superiority of English language and culture, despite her having been born and raised in a solidly Québécois family. She believed in it, and in him, so strongly that she rejected every aspect of her heritage. The only time French was spoken in our home was when my mother and father wanted to keep secrets from us kids. We lived among a million French-speaking people in and around Montreal, but that was irrelevant. If you spoke English well, you were several steps ahead of those who didn't. If you spoke only French, you had better get used to pushing brooms and doing laundry. At my father's factory, no French-Canadian worker ever rose above the level of foreman.

The best route to success for French-Canadian men was within the Catholic Church, which reigned supreme in Quebec when I was a child. And the best route for French-Canadian women was to marry an anglophone man. That was my mother's strategy. She rejected her cultural heritage to become a newly minted anglophone woman, the chatelaine of her home in an anglophone enclave. Mother spoke English with a cultivated hint of an upper-class British accent. Upon first meeting her, no one could believe she had been born in La Belle Province and not on a Cotswold estate. The only vestige she retained of her birthright was her Catholicism.

My mother's only ambition was to be my father's wife, a job that included maintaining a clean, attractive home, cooking his favourite meals, laundering his clothes, and sharing *his* dreams and ambitions. It did not include being the mother of his children. She was, of course. But she resented that responsibility. Mother did not hug her children on any day that I can remember, and although she joined the school's PTA, this represented community service more than family duty. She took no interest in our schooling and no pleasure in our company. This was nothing personal, because she took even less interest in her four grandchildren. I don't offer this as an excuse for what I became. Like other situations confronting us in life, we either deal with it or we do not.

The biggest cliché about patients in psychotherapy concerns their relationship with their mothers. "Tell me about your mother" is a surefire way to start patients plumbing their neuroses. It took me almost fifteen years of therapy to deal with the terrors I suffered as an adolescent. No, I am not going to blame my mother for the faults and the failures in my life. I accept as much blame for them as I take credit for my achievements.

During those therapy sessions, however, I came to realize that my mother adored my father so much that she had no affection left to give to her children. Part of her attitude toward children, and maybe even her upper-class anglophone mannerisms, grew out of nostalgia for the Victorian-era British practice of leaving child-rearing to servants. My mother would have loved to have had a full-time nanny who would free her to spend time doing things she truly enjoyed. Raising children was not one of them.

Between our father's detachment and our mother's disinterest, my sister and my two brothers and I felt like appendages to their relationship. My older brother, Bill, had no interest in education and even less interest in me as his kid brother. My younger brother, Sean, and I were more alike, but it took many years for us to connect in a way that brothers should. My sister, Maureen, always seemed a little lost, somewhat overwhelmed by life.

My strongest recollection as a child is being lonely. I was not lonely in the way an only child might feel, because those children at least can claim a monopoly on their parents' attention. This was worse. This was like growing up among strangers: I lived with people I could not reject because we shared a blood relationship yet could not accept because we all sheathed ourselves within cloaks that defied access.

I refuse to trundle down the Freudian road that leads to blaming my early trail of self-destruction on my family. I wish only to set the stage for all that follows. I was fortunate enough to be raised in a home that provided material comfort and security, an advantage not every child enjoys, as I found out with unbridled horror as an adult. I was unfortunate enough to be in a family incapable of expressing the affection and unrestrained love that children crave. I won some here, I lost some there. And yet, and yet ...

My father loved me. I know he did. He also cherished me as the favourite of his children, an esteem I tested so many times in the most outrageous ways.

MY LIFE HAS BEEN SHAPED, as all lives are, by encounters that I call nudges. None of us proceeds through life without being nudged in this or that direction. Some of these are welcomed, others dreaded. Some lead to success and glory, others to a vomit-drenched alley. Much of this story is about the nudges I received and how well, or how poorly, I handled them. In some cases, *nudge* is an inadequate term. *Shove* doesn't quite do it either. How about *pounce*, *thrust*, and *erupt*? Take your choice. Any sexual connotation you might derive from those terms is intentional.

IT MAY BE MONTRÉAL-OUEST NOW, but in the 1950s and 1960s it was defiantly Montreal West, a ten-block-square enclave nestled between the residential neighbourhood of Notre-Dame-de-Grâce and Ville St. Pierre, once a CPR whistle stop and now one of many communities enfolded within Montreal.

In many ways, life was good in Montreal West during the 1950s. While our parents may have seemed bland and distant, my brothers, sister, and I were surrounded by colourful person-alities. My maternal grandmother, known simply as Mama, was staunchly Québécois, bilingual, and as stubborn and combative as anyone I have ever met. You challenged Mama at the risk of her wrath descending upon you in a frenzy—considered an unseemly response by people as dedicated to anglophone reserve as my parents were. It took Mama to demonstrate the power of passion, though the demonstrations always reflected the darker, angrier side. Still, lessons were lessons, and our periodic visits to Mama's house remain among the clearest memories of my childhood.

Aunt Lisette, my mother's sister, had married a Québécois man named Adrian who was twenty years older than she was. This made him a virtual contemporary of Mama, a situation Mama did not appreciate. The age difference alone might have been enough to generate a loathing between them, but I suspect that Mama resented Aunt Lisette for failing to make as good a "catch" as my mother, who had married an anglophone. This "failure" by Lisette reflected the unspoken second-class citizenship of most French-Canadians at that time.

For the last ten years of her life, before dying at age 101, Mama shared a house in Quebec City with Lisette and her husband. My grandmother frequently remained in her room on the second floor during the day, monitoring Lisette and Adrian's comings and goings on the floor below. Between them was a no man's land as fiercely defended as anything since Vimy Ridge.

Mama and Adrian referred to each other with every insult available in both official languages, and poor Lisette served as the communications link between them. "Tell that old bat upstairs to turn the radio down!" Adrian would shout from the kitchen. Before Lisette could translate this into a more suitable request, my grandmother would bellow down, to the delight of us kids, "That *maudit* ass should mind his own business!" Eavesdropping on conversations between Mama and Uncle Adrian was like watching a real-life episode of *The Honeymooners* or sitting ringside at a World Wrestling Entertainment bout, without the body contact. Their passionate exchanges, as verbally nasty as you can imagine, were a polar opposite of the restraint that was prevalent in my parents' home.

My early years were fairly smooth and uneventful because I did well academically. Breezing through St. Ignatius of Loyola public school, I arrived at Marymount High School in nearby Notre-Dame-de-Grâce fully expecting, as my father did of me also, to enter McGill or some other university and emerge with a degree and a career path. My loneliness intensified during my high school days. Other kids were lonely at times too, but still,

I knew there was something wrong about entering a house where my mother barely acknowledged my presence and my brothers and sisters saw me, as I saw them, as an intrusion. We shared neither secrets nor time.

Only my father, I believed, cared about the things I felt and the secrets I harboured, a conclusion I reached through some sort of osmosis, for he never asked my opinion nor offered his own unless pushed. A quick smile or a soft greeting at the sight of me was sometimes all it took for him to ignite my feelings of affection. He served as a distant hero, an aloof presence and little more, but I clung to it because I needed it, as all boys do.

The most significant lesson my father taught me was the importance of community service. He believed that citizens should take responsibility for their own decisions and actions, and not leave it to government and big business, and he practised what he preached by serving on the Montreal West citizens' council for many years. In this sense, he set a good example for his children. Unfortunately, it also made him even less available to us.

Dad volunteered his services on several election campaigns, and when I was thirteen years old he was involved in yet another one. The local Conservative candidate, a man named Bill Hamilton, had recruited my father to his team. The federal election, held in March of that year, swept John Diefenbaker into power with an enormous majority and marked an historic victory for the Conservative Party. Hamilton, my father's candidate, won a cabinet position and served as the country's postmaster general for several years.

With my father's encouragement, I skipped school on election day and joined him in supporting Hamilton and getting out the vote. Dad suggested I would learn a valuable lesson in politics and share in the electoral excitement. Just as significant to me, I would spend the day in my dad's company, basking in his attention and acknowledgement.

We arrived at campaign headquarters early that morning. Dad went off to join the strategy team in plotting the day's activities. I was instructed to work with a volunteer who was assigned to drive voters to the polling stations in her car. "Hi, I'm Lana," the woman said when we met. "Looks like we're spending the day together." She gave me a warm smile, and we drove away.

In today's vernacular, Lana would be described as hot. About thirty-five or forty years old, she had thick hair, long legs, and large breasts. She seemed inordinately interested in me, expressing keenness in my likes and dislikes in music, sports, and school in a way no adult had done before. I was tall and husky for my age, and I took a good deal of pride in my appearance. Perhaps Lana thought I was much older than my thirteen years. Whatever the attraction, I was naturally flattered by her attention but thought little more of it. She was, after all, almost three times my age.

Dad and I went home for dinner, returning to campaign headquarters after the polls closed. The mood was wild and boisterous. Our candidate had won easily, as had most Conservatives across the country. With every winning Conservative candidate, another cheer swept the crowd and another bottle or two of liquor was opened and passed around. I stood in a corner, sipping a Coke and watching the grown-ups act like children.

Around ten o'clock, as I waited for my father to take me home, I saw Lana tottering toward me, the tottering caused as much by the alcohol she had consumed as by her spike-heeled shoes. We agreed it was a wonderful night and how proud we were about the Conservative Party's success. Then she leaned toward me and whispered, "Come out to my car. I want to show you something."

My father was busy slapping backs and pouring drinks. To the echo of another series of *hurrah!* I followed her outside. We found her car in the parking lot and I climbed into the passenger seat, looking around for whatever it was she wanted to show me. When she started the engine and began to drive away, I asked where we were going. "You'll see," she replied. She looked at me and smiled. "You'll like it."

Lana drove down the street and turned into a laneway that followed the edge of a nearby golf course. The area was dark and deserted, and I began to feel anxious. Finally, she stopped the car among a grove of trees, switched off the engine, and turned to kiss me.

I was too shocked to respond. I had never kissed anyone on the lips before and now this woman, this *older* woman, was probing my mouth with her tongue. In movies and television shows, this tends to be a comic moment, the innocent young boy over-whelmed by an aggressive mature woman. We are expected to laugh, to find humour in this reversal of roles. But reversing the roles does not reduce the fear, the guilt, and the confusion experienced by the youth. Especially the confusion. I was thirteen years old, with hormones about to race through my body, right on schedule. They were responding, but my mind and my heart were not.

This was an older woman, an adult woman, a mother of two—she had told me about her children earlier that day as we ferried voters to the polls—and I had been taught to respect and obey adults. But I had also been taught that this was wrong, a sin in the eyes of God. The experience could have been fulfilling and exhilarating. In truth, it was neither. Unsure what to do, I did nothing.

Lana began fondling me, her hands inside my trousers. She straddled me, one hand fumbling beneath her skirt, and I realized she was removing her panties. I watched, frozen and unbelieving, as she pulled her sweater over her head and removed her bra before pressing herself against me, burying my face in her breasts. My sensation was not of sexual excitement or anticipation but of smothering. I struggled to breathe, to draw air into my lungs. I did not want this to happen; I was not enjoying this act. I simply wanted to escape from this woman and breathe freely again. At one point I feared I would die beneath her, that she might simply push my body from the car, and someone would find my corpse in the morning.

I managed to gasp for air while she moved against me, over and over, there in the darkness of her car. When she was finished I sat drained and totally confused. What had just happened? She slid back behind the steering wheel, where she rearranged her clothes before starting the car's engine. Then, looking across at me, she said, "Don't tell anybody about this, okay? Don't tell a soul. It's our secret."

She asked where I lived, and I gave her my address. In front of my home she flashed me a smile and drove away. It took a long time to find the strength to enter the house. It took even longer to fall asleep that night.

Males are expected, even coached, to be a respectful aggressor in sexual situations. A big difference in age changes everything. Whether it's an older male with a much younger female, or an older woman with a much younger male, especially one as insecure as I was, the experience is traumatic. I know that the act left me feeling confused and guilty.

And it haunts me still. All through my adolescence and into my adult years, right up to middle age, the scars from that experience affected my relationship with women. Only with my wife, Nancy, was I able to overcome the impact of that event. I say this not to excuse my behaviour in the years following the encounter with Lana; I accept complete responsibility for those actions. Yet it is important to understand that a price must be paid whenever an adult steals the innocence of a child, and the payment is always made by the child.

In the weeks after my experience with Lana, I was in a constant maelstrom, my emotions ranging from bitterness and resentment to wonder and a sense of revelation. On a few occasions, I took comfort in the fact that I must be an attractive guy. Lana could have chosen any of the adult men at the campaign headquarters, men with style and power, men who would have known what they were doing, and how to do it. But hey, she had chosen me, thirteen-year-old Frank O'Dea. That must mean *something*.

My ego liked that idea—for a time. Eventually, I began to understand that growing up was a series of discoveries and experiences, and that more important than the nature of these experiences—whether they brought pleasure or pain—was that I have some control over them, some sense that *I* was choosing the place and time to explore them, to absorb the lesson, and to choose whether I was aggressive or compliant.

As much as I needed to deal with all the emotions that occupied me for those few weeks afterward, I could not. In one sense, of course, it had not been an unpleasurable experience. Yet the aftermath was almost torturous. Too embarrassed to discuss it with friends, too inhibited to describe it to my father, I kept the experience hidden, and grew more bewildered than ever. And even more lonely—from that point on, loneliness became my dominant emotion, one that spawned periodic outbursts of anger and recklessness.

Somehow, I discovered Lana's address. Every day, I strolled slowly past her home, waiting perhaps for her to beckon me from her window. She never did, of course. I could have knocked on her door or phoned her, but I chose not to. I don't know why I sought her out in this curious, somewhat passive way. I felt no affection toward her and no urge to repeat the experience. Maybe I was hoping for an explanation, or just wanted to convince myself that it had actually occurred, that it had not been an adolescent dream. Or nightmare.

I was agonized by my inability to share my experience with anyone. Our family was tight-lipped about anything that threatened to disturb our WASPish decorum, and sex certainly qualified. I could not conceive of describing it to teachers or friends, and this inability to share my experience and deal with the emotions it evoked drove me into a state of isolation that grew deeper and darker with time.

I don't know if anyone has clearly identified a trigger that turns some people to alcohol and others away from it. Alcoholics like to blame everyone but themselves, after all. So I refuse to blame Lana for the abyss I began sliding into not long after that night in her car near the golf course. In many ways, she is no more responsible for the thirteen years of alcoholic haze that became my life than the shopkeepers who sold me the beer and wine I craved.

My emotional state is something else, however. The loneliness and alienation I had felt before clambering into the front seat of her car were now sharper and deeper than before. These two emotions are a source of pain and agony just as much as any physical ailment I can name. If you have never felt lonesome among your own family, if you have never felt alienated from those who should be a source of love and comfort, you may not be able to understand this.

The pain becomes so severe and so abiding that you begin to seek relief from any source available. In my case, as has been the case for many, many before me, the source was alcohol. Alcohol provided a release from my unbearable loneliness, because it linked me with others engaged in the same activity, regardless of whether they were friends or strangers.

SUMMERS ARE A SPECIAL TIME FOR KIDS, and our summers were made all the more enjoyable because of the cottage my parents owned in the Laurentians, north of Montreal. The nearest community was a dry town with no bars and no place to buy liquor or beer, and the highlight of each summer weekend was the Saturday night dance. The adults stashed booze in the trunks of their cars; danced inside the hot, crowded hall; and drank outside in the privacy of darkness amid the cool breeze that swept in off the lake.

The summer following my encounter with Lana was my first as a teenager and, like many kids of that age, I was curious about alcohol. My parents, and those of my friends, considered alcohol an essential ingredient in their social life, and we often persuaded some of the adults to give us "just a sip" of their drinks. The adults saw this as a joke, a way of teasing us about the adult experiences that awaited us. We never grew fond of the taste, but we enjoyed the light-headed feeling it generated, and the idea that we were doing something prohibited, something only grown-ups were allowed to do.

Sipping other people's drinks wasn't real drinking, the kind that had some adults bragging about how drunk they had been the previous night. One evening near summer's end, three friends and I pooled our money and persuaded an adult to buy us twelve bottles of Molson's ale and a bottle of lemon gin. The time had come, we decided, to discover once and for all just what alcohol was all about.

Gathering at a remote spot by the water, we initiated ourselves into so-called serious drinking. I have no idea how much I consumed, but it was far more than my share. I had to be carried home by my buddies, throwing up all the way and feeling miserable.

Some people would have seen my experience as a warning to avoid alcohol. My reaction was different. I wanted more.

At the beginning, alcohol satisfied no physical craving in me. In fact, my physical response was, for the most part, repulsion. I never enjoyed the taste of alcohol, never savoured the "fresh malt flavour" of beer, never salivated over the "smoky smoothness" of whisky or appreciated any of those other features dreamed up by smug (and probably sober) advertising copywriters. There was nothing attractive about feeling your stomach preparing to eject its contents, or the blinding headaches that arrived on schedule the next day.

But drinking did provide a sense of belonging, a sense that I was okay because I was among other people doing the same thing, and we appeared to be happy together. I had never truly felt a part of anything—not a part of my family or a part of school, even though I was doing well there. Until I began drinking, I felt I belonged nowhere. Drinking alcohol gave me membership in a group that accepted me. What's more, most of the other members were adults. If adults drank, and I drank too, I owned at least some adult qualities. So why was I wasting time hanging around with kids in a high school?

I also felt that my family expected big things of me, things I doubted I could ever accomplish in life. It's not that I lacked self-confidence; in fact, it was around this time that I boasted to my mother that I would become a millionaire by age thirty-five. It was just that some essential part of my makeup seemed to be missing, preventing me from achieving anything my family was expecting of me, and anything I was expecting of myself. But I didn't know what that piece of personality was, let alone where to find it. I only knew that alcohol filled the space.

My conviction that I was doomed to failure, that I would never amount to anything, isolated me even further from my family and everyone else around me. Alcohol not only filled the space but also the role of that missing piece. While I was drinking with friends, I believed I was capable of doing anything I set my mind to. This was the source of the elation, the rush of measured euphoria, that alcohol and the companionship of drinkers provided. If the price of this pleasure was to throw up at some point, I was willing to pay it.

When I returned to school at the end of that summer, my priorities had shifted. Education no longer mattered. Nothing mattered except getting drunk. By the time I was fourteen, every penny of my allowance, every activity of my day, every thought in my head was directed toward becoming mind-numbingly, stomach-heaving drunk.

It was a relatively easy goal to achieve. In most Quebec communities, beer is sold in grocery stores. Its sale is restricted to adults, of course, but the law, at least at that time, was loosely applied. Rules against selling beer to kids were overlooked by most sales clerks. When I said I was buying the beer for my father, the explanation was almost always accepted, even if I was staggering amid a cloud of alcohol fumes.

The attitude toward drinking was almost as permissive among police officers as among store owners. Nothing illustrates this better than the night I took the beautiful Austin Healey 3000 sports car my father had bought for my mother. Stealing the keys, I roared off to pick up a buddy, stopping first to pick up a few quarts of beer at the grocery store. We tore along the autoroute, each of us with a bottle of beer in our hands. Pulled over by a cop who had clocked me at almost 225 kilometres an hour, I was issued a twenty-dollar speeding ticket and told to "take it easy." Nothing was said about the open bottles of beer, about the obvious fact that we were under age, or about the difficulty each of us had standing upright.

If I believed in guardian angels, I would swear one was watching over me through all those years and all the insane acts

I survived—like the time someone dared me to drive through a toll booth on the autoroute at something over 160 kilometres an hour. Naturally, I did. Amazingly, I survived.

On another occasion I lost control of my Volkswagen Beetle on a back road. I hung on to the steering wheel for dear life as the car vaulted a ditch and struck a young tree that bent almost horizontally to absorb the impact before snapping back and tossing the car onto its roof. The collision broke my nose and left me in a daze. When the Quebec Provincial Police arrived to find me blood-soaked and very drunk, one of the officers demanded, "What were you doing driving a car in your condition?"

I shrugged and replied, "Obviously, I'm too drunk to walk."

I don't remember whether the officer laughed or not. I know he took me to the hospital to be stitched up, then sent me home. Again, no charges were laid. That was the temper of the times. Drunk driving may have been illegal, but it did not carry the stigma it does today. Jaywalking and littering were illegal as well, after all.

Perhaps I can attribute my relative good fortune to the fact that I was usually driving very late at night, on my way to or from one of the various bars that sold liquor out the back door after closing hours. Even then, I failed to avoid serious incidents, such as the time several friends and I were driving much too fast, and much too drunk, along the highway. Without warning, we came upon two cars that had just collided and were sitting, steaming and crumpled, in the middle of the road. On impact, my friend's head went through the windshield of our car. That was disastrous enough, but suddenly all three cars were on fire, and I barely managed to pull his head back and drag him out of the wreckage before flames engulfed us. He endured 123 stitches—you don't forget a statistic like that when you've seen the horrific cuts on a friend's face—but we both survived. Although I wasn't driving the car when the collision occurred, we were all equally drunk and equally responsible.

Guilt always arrived in the morning without fail and without mercy. I would awaken with a remembrance of the previous evening's occurrences and the weight of remorse on my shoulders. "What have I done?" was my first thought, quickly followed by, "I'll never do it again." But, of course, I did.

The cost was horrendous no matter how you measure it. The boy I had become, the one who breezed through public school with high marks, spent three years in grade ten because he couldn't function as a student or, in many ways, as a human being. Alcohol had become the most important thing in my life. I had no interest in school, no interest in sports, and not much interest in girls. I thought only of drinking and of the comfort it provided. If there was no liquor to be had at home, there was always money: I stole from my father's wallet, my mother's purse, my brother's piggy bank, anywhere there was cash. When the theft was discovered, everyone knew who had taken the money. In the beginning, I denied being a thief. Later I simply shrugged off the accusations. Each time I felt humiliated, as I do today just recalling it. *But I did not stop.*

Many people tried convincing me that I needed to change. They cared about me and expressed their concern, but I didn't hear them. I *refused* to hear them. Alcohol had become my only reason to exist. The need to get drunk occupied my mind from the moment I woke up sober until I had consumed enough alcohol to blot out everything except the joy and relief it brought me.

My father finally placed me in a private school where he could effectively buy me a high school diploma. This should have been a positive move. Instead, it proved a complete failure.

The problem was not with the school or with its teachers, who did their best to set me straight and provide an education. No, the problem was the school's location: around the corner from the cozy Monkland Tavern. The tavern's owners were willing to serve a tall and husky sixteen-year-old with money to spend and a thirst for beer. I looked and acted old enough to drink and, in those distant days, that was all the criteria they needed.

Over the years that I drank alcohol, I loved everything about bars. Walking into a dark, smoky bar brought me a sense of contentment and belonging even before I had my first drink. I loved the characters who inhabited bars, the stories they traded, and the lies they told. I loved the contradiction of refuge and risk that bars provided, the sight of liquor bottles stacked on the shelves, the gales of laughter and shouts of anger, the smiles and the tears on faces I had never seen before and usually never saw again.

Nothing about the Monkland was attractive or even memorable beyond that I could escape within its secure atmosphere. I remember the dim lighting, the square shape of the room, the beer taps on the bar and the rows of bottles behind it, the muted television sets mounted on the wall, the posters showing brands of beer, and the wooden chairs and tables. Whenever I approached the Monkland, I savoured the anticipation of entering the place with confidence, sliding onto the stool, and accepting the first beer. I remember nothing of the people behind the bar, the people seated at the tables, or the people sharing the bar area. With one chilling exception.

Almost every day at lunchtime and after school, I perched myself on a stool in the tavern and inhaled as much beer as the cash in my pockets could buy. I still didn't enjoy the taste. I became a regular, a kid who should have been on a baseball diamond or at a hockey rink, sitting on a bar stool laughing, drinking, and feeling like he belonged.

One day after school I was in the tavern, smiling and satisfied. I was in the warm sanctuary of the Monkland. I was drinking a beer. I was at ease.

A Montreal West police officer slid onto the stool next to me, ordered himself a beer, and smiled in my direction. He said he thought he recognized me and asked my father's name. I told him. He must have recognized the name, since my father was serving on town council, which oversaw the police force. Besides, Montreal West was compact enough that everyone knew who both my father and the officer were. He was your classic beefy cop, over six feet tall with thick red hair and the swagger that some police officers acquire. He introduced himself. Let's call him Murphy.

We began talking about nothing in particular. Murphy was funny and entertaining, and I was impressed that a police officer found me interesting enough to engage me in conversation. He bought me a drink, then another, and another. Finally, he offered me a ride home. I agreed, of course; it was a good idea considering how drunk I was. A cop, one of the good guys, would make sure I got home safely. How could I refuse? I followed him to his car, got in, leaned my head back, and closed my eyes. I was going home. I was drunk and feeling good and going home.

But when I opened my eyes, we weren't at my house. We were at his. He invited me inside under some pretence that I didn't question and, once inside, he raped me. His hands were on me like Lana's had been, but this time things were different. This time, I was too drunk to resist with more than words. This time, my hormones were not responding with excitement and discovery but with fear and repulsion. And this time, it hurt. It hurt terribly.

I was there in body but not in mind, wanting only for it to be finished, to be completed, to end. When it did, my reactions were similar to those I had felt after the attack in the car that night a few years earlier: confusion, guilt, fear, and, this time, betrayal. I had been attacked by a police officer, a figure I had been taught since childhood to respect and trust.

I don't know if I cried afterward. I don't know if Murphy apologized or warned me not to talk about it. I just know that eventually he drove me home, leaving me in the dark outside my house, shivering, silent, and traumatized.

Again, I told no one. I had told no one about Lana either, though I had made a point of seeking out her house, perhaps hoping that she would explain things. I had no interest in finding Murphy again. I wanted only to forget what had happened. But, of course, I could not. My experience with Lana left me feeling confused. My experience with Murphy humiliated me. That humiliation was still gnawing at me several days later when, one evening after dinner, the telephone rang.

I recognized the voice immediately. It was Murphy. Was I coming to meet him at the Monkland Tavern? Or maybe I'd rather come to his house. After all, he said, I knew where he lived. I blurted out some answer, anything just to end the call. Then I sat alone for a very long time, shivering with fright.

For days afterward, each time the telephone rang, I feared it was Murphy. He was a police officer. He could do anything he wanted to me, and who would stop him? Who would protect me? Only one person could. My father. I needed Dad to know. I needed him to protect me and end it.

One evening, I asked Dad if I could speak to him in private. We entered the darkened living room, Dad asking, "What's up? What's the big secret?"

I sat nervously on the sofa. My father closed the door, sat across from me, and waited for me to begin. It took a long time to get started, but I finally asked Dad if he knew Murphy. When Dad said he did, I began telling him what had happened to me. I described Murphy entering the tavern and sitting on the stool beside me. I explained how he had been friendly, buying me drinks, telling me stories, making me laugh, making me feel comfortable and trusting with him. I said Murphy had offered to drive me home, and I accepted. Hadn't it been a good idea to accept a ride home with a police officer? Had I done something wrong by riding with him in his car and following him into his house for a minute, just a stop on the way home?

My father sat listening with no response, without an expression of any kind, until I began describing how Murphy had attacked me, how he overpowered me and forced me onto his bed. I told Dad how Murphy had been too strong for me to fight off, even when he began removing my clothes. I started to tell of the things Murphy had done to me and how I had screamed for him to stop, and at that point Dad grew pale. Becoming more uncomfortable with every word I spoke, he looked as though some parasite was gnawing inside him. I pressed on, wanting my father to understand what I had gone through and how violated I felt, how much I needed him to listen and react, and how afraid I was when Murphy called our house, wanting to see me, and that he would do it again.

Before I could implore my father to do something, anything to make me feel good about myself and safe from another attack, he did something that stunned me. He shook his head, rose from his chair, and walked out of the room, leaving me tearful and alone.

[T W O]

For the Good
of the Family

After my father left the room, I wasn't angry, only remorseful. I was messing up my own life, and now I was ruining my father's by telling him of Murphy's sexual attack. Perhaps I should have said nothing and avoided upsetting him. Perhaps in some ways I was as much to blame for upsetting Dad as Murphy's actions were.

Dad's decision to walk away physically and emotionally from the news of the sexual assault, and from the deeper problems I faced, did not give me licence to do the things I did or become the person I became over the next several years. Yet the cumulative effect of those three instances—my encounter with Lana, Murphy's attack, and Dad's inability to help me deal with my pain—left scars on my psyche that I'm still dealing with today. How could they not? For years afterwards, I found it difficult to maintain a normal relationship with either men or women. Could

I trust any of them? Could I trust myself, since I suffered the guilt syndrome that many rape victims experience? It took many years of therapy, introspection, and forgiveness—forgiving both my father and myself—before those scars began to fade.

I never erased the sight of Dad walking away from me, however. It pained me then and it pains me now. I suppose I could argue that my actions in later years were an attempt to attract his attention, to scream in some manner, "Look at me, deal with me, acknowledge who and what I am, what these people made me become!" I was never able to do this because, I suppose, I loved my father too much, and I already felt guilty about hurting him in so many ways for such a long time. Nor did I reach any conclusion along the lines of, "He doesn't give a damn about me, so why should I?"

The ten years after Murphy's attack resemble, for me, a long, inexorable train wreck, one that I witnessed as both passenger and conductor.

Over the years, I was involved in seventeen incidents with my parents' cars, including one that turned my mother's beloved and beautiful Austin Healey 3000 into a pile of rubble. Each time, I took the car without their permission to pursue yet another night of drinking, another night of skidding into a lamppost, into a ditch, into another car. I once woke my father at three in the morning to tell him that I had crashed his car, that my friend was in the hospital with broken ribs, that a taxi driver was waiting downstairs to be paid for bringing me home, and that he had better get up and deal with the situation.

I took no pride in upsetting my father this way. I disliked hurting him. The next morning, after sobering up and realizing what I had done, I felt the usual immense guilt. Whatever my father's failings, he did not deserve being treated this way. I knew it, and I felt badly about it. But I couldn't seem to stop myself.

I encountered other kinds of wreckage as well. I became prey to almost every kind of sexual deviant. At times I felt as though I were wearing an invitation on my forehead, a sign visible to sexual predators that said "Attack me!" Something in my demeanour and my words and actions had changed in ways I did not then understand, and do not fully understand to this day.

My attackers included two priests. Both exploited my deference to authority and my gratitude toward anyone who provided me with alcohol.

In his endless effort to secure a high school education for me and perhaps even to remove me from the Monkland Tavern and the threat of Murphy, Dad enrolled me at St. Lawrence College, a private school in Quebec City. I boarded there during the week, returning home to Montreal on weekends. One Friday afternoon, a priest at the school told me he was driving to Montreal that evening; would I like a ride with him rather than having to sit on the bus for hours? Of course I would. After all, I could trust a priest.

When we arrived in Montreal, the priest invited me up to his hotel room for a drink, and I accepted. We had one drink and then another. He was a priest, for goodness' sake. I had been betrayed by a cop, but what would I fear from a man who celebrated Mass, who sat on the other side of the confessional? I had been brought up to show deference to authority, especially that of the Church. It was still several years before stories of child abuse involving priests and boys became public. My trust in the Church and all that it represented remained absolute. And so, when it became obvious that the priest was interested not in my soul but in my body, the guilt resurfaced. I assumed that I had done something wrong, that *I* had been the one who sinned by tempting him to do what he was doing. Why else would it happen?

A different man, a different car, a different room, but the same horror and humiliation, the same resolve not to tell anyone about the experience, out of fear, out of guilt, out of shame.

As essential as trust may be to a child, it is also immensely fragile. Once shattered, it cannot be easily repaired or rebuilt. Three pillars that I had honoured, respected, and depended on— my father, a police officer, and a priest—had betrayed that trust in the most devastating ways imaginable.

When it was over, when we were dressed and back in the priest's car, when we were entering my neighbourhood of Montreal West, I remained inert in the way that a rock is inert. I was unfeeling, unsettled, and immobile.

A few months later, I was introduced to another priest, this one the uncle of a friend. "The old guy's an alcoholic," my friend whispered to me. It was a family joke, I suppose. It was no joke, however, when I accepted the priest's invitation to share a drink with him, followed by another. This time, my horror and surprise were muted. This time, it seemed inevitable. A priest shows interest, he suggests a drink, and then another and another, and somewhere, at some time, his hands will be on me and for the next several minutes I will be there with him and yet very distant.

I will keep asking myself in the midst of the experience, Why? Why me? Why here? Why this?

I was unable to feel totally victimized. I could not find it in my heart to blame Lana or Murphy or either of the two priests. I always blamed myself for drinking, for being foolish, for just being me. Always. And that is why I was never vengeful. The fault lay not with my attackers. It lay entirely with me. That is what I believed.

My feelings for the second priest were more of sympathy than anger. He was, after all, a tragic figure, a man driven by his own desires, by loneliness, by a loss of faith perhaps, to break one of the most inviolable laws of both the Church and secular society.

I discussed none of these incidents with anyone. Certainly not with my father, given his reaction when I told him of the attack by Murphy. I locked the raw, pent-up emotions within me, where they grew corrosive. If I had been wild before these encounters, now I grew even wilder, prepared to be as out of control as I chose.

Self-centred and isolated, I was oblivious to my mother's reaction to my behaviour, and that of my brothers and sister. As time passed, their opinions proved of little interest to me anyway, though I dearly wished my father would try to understand me, to help me, to display his love for me. In reflection now, I am sure that he tried, but it was simply beyond his capability. No matter how dedicated he might have been to flying by flapping his arms, he would be just as incapable of providing the understanding and expressing his love for me. It was simply not in him to do so.

With time, my family ceased to be part of my world, which remained encompassed within the next bottle of beer, the next glass of liquor, the next alcohol-induced sensation of being isolated from the lives of others except those whose company I shared while drinking. I constructed my own world, one that I entered and inhabited when drunk. It was a lonely and difficult place, but once I reached it, I wanted to remain there.

I managed to abuse and alienate most of the few friends I had, even though I desperately needed people to like me, people I could trust. My mistreatment of friends took many forms. I stole money from them to buy alcohol, I abused their hospitality, and in my confused state I tried to become sexually active with some, both male and female. I don't know what they thought of me when that happened. I don't know what I thought of myself.

It is impossible to exaggerate how confused I was feeling. I had never thought I was gay, yet a police officer, two priests, and others had attacked me. I must be homosexual, then, otherwise why would this be happening to me? But what had attracted Lana to me? How could that have happened? I went back and forth on this issue in a way that only adolescents can do, without understanding or resolution.

I asked myself if I was living a lie by thinking I was *not* gay. If I was, wouldn't sexual relations with other males be a method of making friends, of finally dissolving this intense loneliness I was feeling? And shouldn't I know for sure?

Those who have no doubt of their sexuality, or at least no reason to doubt it, may find this a bit of a stretch. Most people respond with firm conviction to any query about their sexual preference. Whether they are objectively correct in their response is another matter. But the majority of people are not raped by both sexes in their critical formative years, nor do they discover that the one source of solace that should always be available turns his back on them, choosing to pretend no problem exists, choosing to walk away in silence.

It took years of therapy and inner reflection to deal with these issues. As I discovered over those years, the only way to deal with them was to accept them. There is no turning back, no reassessment to be made, and no reward for pretence or rejection. I am what I am today, and I was what I was back then. If it is difficult to comprehend how and why I could engage in some of the things I did through my adolescent years and beyond, I can assure you that it was even more difficult for me to understand them.

The overwhelming emotion during those years, the one that dominated every waking hour, was not anger, as my experience might suggest. It was fear. I remained fearful of whatever else was about to happen in my life. At its heart, I feared the unknown. I feared the things that I could neither know nor prevent, but instead of cowering in a corner and withdrawing from the world, I threw myself at it, thus precipitating many of the things I feared. Alcohol certainly played a role, but it did not bolster my courage nearly as much as it dissolved my fear.

The danger I presented to myself, and to those I encountered, haunts me to this day. People have told me I'm lucky to be alive, and I suppose it's true. My response, however, is that I'm even luckier that others are also alive. I would do anything during those years to obtain alcohol, anything to experience that first notion of escape and the warmth it provided. This led to many appalling incidents, most recalled through the dim haze of alcohol and time. But one stands out relatively clearly.

It was summertime, and a friend, fool that he was, loaned me his rear-engine Chevrolet Corvair to drive to a party in the suburbs. The party was fuelled by alcohol, and as midnight approached I discovered that the supply was almost depleted. Only midnight and already out of booze? It was unthinkable.

I knew a "blind pig"—a bar that sold alcohol out the back door—in the next town. If I drove fast enough, I could get there before it closed. When I suggested this, everyone thought it was a good idea, especially me. I would buy the beer and liquor we needed and save the party. I would be a hero to my friends. More important, I'd be able to stay drunk longer.

I drove off alone in my friend's Corvair, a car whose tricky handling was made famous by Ralph Nader in his book *Unsafe at Any Speed*. Rounding a curve on the highway at about a hundred kilometres an hour, the car proved Nader right when its rear end swung into the oncoming lane and clipped a car passing in the other direction. I don't know what happened to the other car, or its driver and passengers. I was too busy regaining control of the swerving and swaying Corvair, trying to keep it out of the ditch and pointed in the direction I was going. Besides, nothing really mattered except reaching the bar in time. The Corvair was still driveable, I was unhurt, and the blind pig might be closing in minutes. So I kept going, nursing the battered car to the bar, not even looking back. It was important to keep going. It was important that I knew how to get the alcohol, that I would bring it back for my friends and me to consume, and that I would continue to belong, to be appreciated, to fit in with the crowd.

I bought the booze and staggered back to the car with only a glance at its battered side. Everyone at the party greeted me with joy. We drank on and on. Somehow, in the darkness of the night and the dimness of my memory, I made it home without incident.

The police arrived at our front door early the next morning and charged me with impaired driving and leaving the scene of an accident. Handcuffed and fingerprinted, I was tossed in jail. The clang of the cell door closing behind me echoed in my head for hours. This was no dormitory-style accommodation, no gentle treatment for under-age offenders. This was serious incarceration, an environment that was intentionally dehumanizing. I was locked in a cell that could barely contain the steel cot that had no mattress, the dirty toilet that had no seat, and the rusty sink that had no hot water. The concrete walls had no windows. When I was permitted out of my cell, I encountered street characters as rough as any portrayed on film. But I feared them less than I did the prison guards, who treated the prisoners as though we were obstinate cattle, constantly prodding and demeaning us. By this time, I had good reason to be wary of authority figures.

The experience should have changed me, but it didn't. Dad bailed me out, then hired an expensive lawyer to defend me in court. The lawyer's strategy was simple and effective. "We have proof that the car in question struck another vehicle and continued without stopping," he argued in fine, mellifluous style. "And we have proof that my client had temporary possession of the vehicle that evening. We do not have proof, however, that my client was behind the wheel at the time of the collision, so he must remain innocent." The judge agreed, and the Crown attorney settled for my pleading guilty to a charge of impaired driving.

Struck by the cynicism of the law and impressed by my own role as the guy who stood in the spotlight while the officers of the court, in all their pomposity, made weighty decisions, I walked out of the courtroom elated. Within a few hours I was celebrating my success—at the bar.

I can only guess what my friends and their families thought of me during those years. I know that I was lonely, as lonely as anyone can possibly feel. St. Lawrence, the school in Quebec City, eventually gave up on me. When it did, Dad found another private school, one so lenient and permissive that it eventually handed me a high school graduation diploma. My father's money was more responsible for that piece of paper than anything I did to earn it.

Having expressed his concern for me in the only way he knew how, my father offered a deal. If I spent a year at a demanding job, one that demonstrated how hard some people had to work to make a living, he would pay for my college education. I agreed, and for a year worked in the CPR locomotive yards. The job gave me insight into the desperate mindset of many working people.

It was my first exposure to men who hated their jobs and, in some ways, hated themselves for spending such large chunks of their lives at something they despised. Much of the work was tough physical labour, and I remember the older workers literally counting down the years—"seven more and I'm outta here"—until they could retire. Perhaps their bleak prospects and hopelessness affected me. Although they sought solace and release from their misery in drink, and I joined them from time to time, the experiences were not memorable because they simply were not enjoyable. Drinking represented rebellion and camaraderie to me, a sense of "us against the world and to hell with them all!" To those locomotive workers, alcohol represented neither a stimulant nor liberation. It was merely a sedative.

Finally, my year of penance at hard labour was completed. I should have been overjoyed when Dad announced that he had managed to get me into a college. A higher education would liberate me from a life spent amid the hell of the men I had met in the locomotive yard. I might have been expected to buckle down and seize the opportunity. But again, I did not.

The school wasn't Yale or McGill or anything so prestigious. In fact, it was the only one that, based on my school records, would accept me. I set off from Montreal West to become a freshman at the South Dakota School of Mines and Technology. With luck and hard work, I would become a mining engineer whose brilliance and ability would be in demand around the globe.

By the end of the first semester, both the school and I agreed that I had no future either in mining or in South Dakota. When he got the news, Dad sent money for me to buy an airline ticket home. I cashed the ticket, bought passage on a bus, and spent the difference on booze. After the bus pulled into Montreal, it took half an hour of panhandling to get a dime for the pay phone. I called Dad and asked him to meet me at the bus terminal and take me home. My formal education had ended.

I managed to get a job driving a delivery truck for a large local dairy, which sounds like a safe occupation. And it was, as long as

I was working. The problems began at the end of the day when many of the drivers gathered at Peg's, a nearby saloon as rough as any biker bar you're likely to step into.

Peg's was attached to a cheap motel, most of the rooms occupied by hookers who spent their vertical hours in the bar, either taking it easy or looking for customers. Chico, Peg's bartender, tried to keep everybody in line by the strength of his presence—he looked like a grizzly with a migraine—and the weight of his nightstick, a length of two-by-four that he swung like a Montreal Expos baseball player in the warm-up circle.

It was a dark, smoky, dangerous place, and the danger appealed to my wild side. The floor was constantly wet with spilled beer, vomit, and occasionally blood, and the jukebox in the corner blasted country-and-western music about people being betrayed by their lovers, having their pickup truck repossessed, and watching their dog die.

What with the music, the alcohol, the hookers, and the excessive testosterone, fist fights broke out over a single ill-spoken phrase or even an innocent glance. Once the donnybrook started, chairs were smashed over heads and bottles were tossed at windows, until Chico and his nightstick restored order.

The bar was a place to lose my persistent loneliness. Naturally, I felt at home there.

Many of the dairy drivers couldn't wait to reach Peg's after a day's work, which led to bitter competition among those of us who were serious drinkers and preferred to duck flying bottles than relax with our families at home. The sooner you finished your deliveries and returned to the office, the sooner you could start drinking at Peg's. Returning even five minutes ahead of the other guy could mean that you left the dairy as much as an hour earlier than him—giving you an extra hour of drinking. Everyone wanted to be the first to reach the office, cash in the day's receipts, unload the truck, return product to inventory, and complete all the other details that brought the workday to a close. This incentive to arrive ahead of other drivers led to outlandish behaviour.

One day while driving well over the speed limit, racing to be first back at the office, I spotted another dairy truck ahead of me. I pressed the accelerator to the floor and caught up with it, but the other driver matched my speed and soon we were two heavy trucks racing abreast on a busy four-lane highway, driving recklessly just to gain a few extra minutes in a bar. I ended the race by reaching behind my seat, grabbing a box of eggs, and tossing it at the other truck's windshield, where the eggs splattered into an opaque mess that effectively blinded the driver. He was forced to pull over to clean the glass while I sped off, laughing all the way.

I thrived in the dingy bar atmosphere. I relished the darkness, content to spend my days consuming as much alcohol as possible among people with the same limited ambition. We weren't interested in throwing darts, watching sports events, or indulging in any other distraction from our intention of getting drunk in the company of others.

At Peg's, there was always the chance, the likelihood even, of frayed tempers exploding into a drunken brawl. I remember little about the details, and anyway, there would be too many to recount. One element, however, was consistent among all the fights, and that was the fear that contorted the face of the first person to be struck a solid blow or knocked to the floor. Bar fights are not like the scuffles depicted in movies and on TV. The real thing tends to be explosive, violent, and frightening. To be on the receiving end of a blow from a fist, a chair, or a beer bottle is to immediately comprehend both your mortality and your stupidity for engaging in the brawl.

No one who suffered one of these blows responded immediately with pain or anger. The first reaction was always abject fear, born of the realization that the next blow could kill them. The fear appeared on their faces and was felt in their hearts. It was visceral and disturbing in a way that no false bravado or alcohol can conceal. I know, because sometimes it was me on Peg's floor, looking up at the twisted, angry face of the man who had just struck me, and dreading what was about to happen next.

AFTER THE DAIRY AND I AGREED that I was unsuited for the job, I drifted through a series of other positions, some rewarding and interesting, others mind-numbing and tedious. Among the more promising was a job with Northern Electric installing switching stations at various locations in Quebec. The position came with a car allowance, which I used to finance a new vehicle, plus an expense account, and a chance to explore new bars and swap stories with other employees while sliding into an alcoholic haze.

Some days we drank to drown our sorrows. Other days we drank to float our joy. One instance of the dark humour we traded involved a pamphlet the company had distributed to its employees. The folder included a test to determine if you were an alcoholic. My drinking buddies and I thought this was a big joke, and we met at our favourite bar to take the test, reading the questions aloud to each other and competing for the most hilarious answers. *Do you lose time from work due to drinking?* Sure as hell try to! *Is drinking affecting your reputation?* What damn reputation? *Do you drink alone?* Not if we can help it. *Were we alcoholics?* Hell, no. Well, maybe yes. Hey, so what? Let's have another drink.

Through all these experiences, I felt there was more. Not just more to life than sitting in a bar—that was obvious. I felt there was more to *me*; that I happened to be in the wrong place at the wrong time. I was certain that at some point one of those two factors—either place or time—would change, and I would finally learn how much more of me there was.

This conviction, this belief in myself, made me arrogant at times. I would insult those around me, leading to charges that I was "too big for my britches" and often ending in fist fights with drinking buddies. Yet I never felt superior to my bar mates. If anything, I continued to harbour familiar feelings of guilt, shame, and humiliation.

Nevertheless, I did believe that there was more somewhere. More of what, I didn't know. But at some point I would discover an end to the kind of life I was living, and the others would not. That is what I believed.

I had inherited my father's interest in politics and I volunteered at candidates' offices during provincial and federal elections. I enjoyed the competitiveness and the drama of an election campaign, as well as the feeling that I was working on something bigger than me, fulfilling a citizen obligation. Well, that sounds like a good thing to say, but my concept of working on behalf of my country and community was a sham. My real incentive was alcohol. I knew drinks were always available at political meetings, parties, and receptions. I worked hard, but only as hard as I needed to toast our anticipated success with drinks paid for by others.

In spite of this alcoholic handicap, I built a reputation for campaign savvy and, in recognition of my political skills and instincts, in 1965 I won the job of managing an electoral office for an up-and-coming political newcomer named Pierre Elliott Trudeau. Although I cannot honestly claim enough prescience to predict the spectacular political future awaiting him, I was taken with his intelligence and political *savoir faire*, and on the day Trudeau entered the office I was managing, thrust out his hand, and said, "You must be Frank O'Dea," I was as smitten as anyone.

How different things might have been if I had clung to Trudeau's coattails and ridden with him to political glory. My responsibilities included handling campaign funds, and my life might have changed in many ways if I had kept out of the cash drawer. When my colleagues discovered that I had pilfered money to buy liquor—what else?—I was kicked off the team.

I am convinced that I was waiting to be rescued or, as I would realize in rare moments of honesty and lucidity, waiting to find the strength to rescue myself. The bars, the drunkenness, the often total disregard for anything beyond the next drink, were markers on the road to something different.

I remembered reading the biography of William Zeckendorf, the flamboyant U.S. developer who was single-handedly responsible for revitalizing much of Manhattan (he developed the site of the UN Building); Washington D.C.; Denver; and other cities. During his career, Zeckendorf made and lost immense fortunes, riding high as one of the world's wealthiest men one month and running from creditors the next.

In spite of his periodic failures, he kept achieving success by turning his unique vision into splendid realities. It was Zeckendorf who proposed, in the 1950s, the idea of underground cities radiating out from railroad stations serving the suburbs of large metropolitan areas. The concept was much too radical for Toronto, where he first presented it. When Toronto politicians sniffed that it was too expensive and impractical, Zeckendorf carried it down the road to Montreal, which responded to the idea with enthusiasm. The result of Zeckendorf's vision was Place Ville Marie, a development that kicked off a revitalization of Montreal's core and still stands as a triumphant symbol of the city's vision. Although underground cities were eventually built in Toronto and other North American metropolises, many people believe no one has done it better than Place Ville Marie and Zeckendorf.

The strength of Zeckendorf's conviction was enormous. To transform his ideas into reality, he risked and at times lost everything he had, staying just a few dollars ahead of the sheriff before sinking into bankruptcy. He recovered a portion of his wealth before he died, but it almost didn't matter. He started with nothing, acquired hundreds of millions of dollars (on paper at least), and altered some of the most famous corners of the world. That was Zeckendorf's lesson to me: No matter where you begin or where you finish, you can do amazing things with your life if you choose to.

In the back of my mind, somewhere behind the alcohol-induced clouds, I always believed I would emulate Zeckendorf one way or another. I doubted I would create my own Place Ville Marie or be acclaimed one of the great urban visionaries, but when the time came and when the circumstances were right, I would pull off a mini-Zeckendorf. In the meantime, I needed a drink.

THINGS AT HOME were becoming intolerable. My parents dreaded that the next late-night call, the next drunken collision with a lamppost, would produce not a visit to the police station to bail me out but a trip to the morgue to identify my body. I found my family just as unbearable as they found me. Bill, Sean, and Maureen avoided me whenever they could and feared bringing their friends to the house in case I embarrassed them with my drunken antics. All of this isolated me even further from my family, and when Dad joined a friend to launch their own business in Quebec City and the rest of the family went along, I remained in Montreal.

I had made friends somewhere along the way with a great guy named Jacques Lemieux. About my age but with a much beefier physique, Jacques worked as a bailiff, a highly respected position in Quebec society. His duties included seizing property from people who neglected to pay their bills. The goods were usually furniture, television sets, and cars, and the situations were often heart-rending—I know, because I accompanied Jacques on some of these assignments. With the physique of a professional foot-ball linebacker, Jacques's mere presence made his job a little easier, but he was no thug. In fact, he was a gentleman, in the formal and informal senses of the word. No matter what the circumstances were, Jacques was always respectful and even almost apologetic to the people whose goods he was seizing. Many cases upset him, though he hid it well. Later, he might confide to me how badly he felt for the people who had just watched their furniture or their refrigerator or television set being driven away. Jacques knew that often it was not their fault. When you are out of work, your priorities for food and shelter override the obligation to pay your monthly bills.

Jacques's observations made an impact on me, and I grew sharply aware of society's underclass, and how many of its members find themselves in a cycle of defeat.

When I told Jacques about my family moving to Quebec City and my reluctance to join them, he invited me to move in with his family. This proved a revelation, a bright and positive interlude in an otherwise dark and obscure period of my life.

The Lemieuxs were a startling contrast to my family. Raymond, the father and a CBC-TV producer, was a man of talent and erudition. A Québécois, he married a delightful Irish woman and they filled their home with six wonderful kids. Among their children were Pete, who lived and breathed automobiles, and the eldest boy Robert, a lawyer who acted on behalf of the FLQ separatist party. The parents were avowed federalists.

Settling into a spare bunk in the boys' room, I became a pseudo-member of the family, though I rarely joined the debates about federalism versus separatism that often began at the dinner table and avalanched into the living room through the rest of the evening.

The incisive views and deep passion that were evident in the discussions astonished me. In my family, emotions weren't merely held in check, they were denied. Revealing your deepest feelings, whether through tears, shouts, or unrestrained laughter, was considered déclassé, the kind of thing others did. We were not other people, of course; we were Anglo-Canadian.

The Lemieuxs, however, fulfilled all the clichés expected from people with a blend of Irish temper and French-Canadian joie de vivre. Nothing was held back, including their love for each other, which no one questioned. A conversation might begin with a comment about a television interview with Pierre Trudeau, or a speech delivered by René Lévesque, or the price of a good steak, and soon Trudeau or Lévesque or the cattle farmer was being hailed as either a hero or tyrant. Voices were soon raised in anger, fists slammed onto tables, statistics quoted and refuted, and not an inch was given until things cooled down, as they inevitably did. And when political points of view were not being tossed back and forth like artillery fire, hugs and kisses were being exchanged with sincere and open affection, while I stood to one side, absorbing it all with amazement.

When the topic of such passionate arguments was Quebec separatism, the experience provided an insight into the true nature of Canada's two solitudes. The parents argued on behalf of federalism, citing economic realities. In response, Robert defended separatism as a cultural imperative. I saw the Lemieux family as a microcosm of everything this country deals with at every functional level, and the arguments were both heartening and distressing to watch. Those on each side knew, I suspect, that they could never win the other side over, a realization that did not prevent them from launching the same volleys over and over again. How, I wondered, can we settle these kinds of arguments across the country when there is no hope of finding agreement within one family? And how could anyone rationalize such intense personal attacks one day and openly express affection the next?

Some things did distract the family from politics, thank goodness. Peter's fascination with cars included motor racing, and while I was living with them the family bought an MGB sports car. Given Peter's dedication to the sport and the family's intense competitiveness, the car did not remain a street machine for long. Peter set it up for racing, and we spent much of that summer trucking it north to events at Mont-Tremblant and south to races at Watkins Glen in New York State. While I worked in the pits (and drank beer), the drivers lined up at the starting line and tore down the track among Porsches, Triumphs, Jaguars, and other cars, the drivers speeding as recklessly on the racetrack sober as I had driven drunk on the autoroute.

I wish I could say we scored victories here and there, but the truth is that we never finished a race. Crashes or mechanical problems kept plaguing us, and we spent a lot of time in the pits. The mechanical challenges were not a reflection of Peter's skill, because he was gifted when it came to tuning and repairing a car. We simply couldn't afford all the specialized parts and materials it took to keep the car running under the stress of racing. Yet we never gave up entirely either. Although we never felt the ecstasy of winning a race, we enjoyed the sense of participating and tapping a reservoir of hope. And that, of course, was a lesson in itself.

As enjoyable as this sojourn with the Lemieux family was, it did not eliminate my thirst for alcohol. I continued to drink whenever and wherever I could, and if the Lemieuxs sensed I had a drinking problem, they politely avoided talking about it.

Those months with the Lemieux family opened a window on a life I had not experienced before. I realized that families can express affection and support for each other. They can encourage and tolerate each other's points of view, listen with empathy to the fears and ambitions of family members, and provide a refuge where no pain or problem was too challenging, too outrageous, or too painful to be addressed.

I carried those new-found values home with me when my family returned to Montreal and my stay at the Lemieuxs' ended. After sampling so much warmth and openness, I found the coolness of my family even more stifling than before, and I grew quietly furious about it. My drinking and rebellion resumed, this time tinged with a rage I had never revealed before. I took joy in shocking my brothers and sister, in defying the wishes of my parents, and in watching family members cringe at the sight of me.

The final straw involved, once again, a car. This time it was not my father's, nor even my own. When I left Northern Electric, I had kept the car I had bought for my job but damaged it in a collision with a tree. While it was being repaired, I drove a rental car. The rental company, having checked my driving record, refused to provide me with a vehicle without a guarantee from my father. It took a good deal of persuading, but Dad finally gave in and promised to be responsible should I have an accident.

Two weeks later, the rental company called to demand its car back. I had failed to return it for good reason: It was a wreck. I had bounced off something, likely a bridge abutment, while driving drunk. I managed to pull off the road and into a parking lot where I abandoned the car, taking a cab home. My own car was ready the next day anyway. Why deal with the hassle of explaining things to the rental company?

After Dad settled things, he called me into the living room and asked me to sit down because he had something important to say. "Frank," he said, "for the good of the family, you have to go."

I didn't have to ask, "Go where?" I knew the meaning of his words. I even acknowledged to myself that I had been forcing him to make this decision for years. When I remained silent, he went on as though he needed to justify his decision.

"I'm tired of getting calls in the middle of the night to pick you up or bail you out of jail." His words were delivered not with sorrow or anger but with resignation. I was, after all, his favourite child. "I'm tired of you stealing money from everyone to buy alcohol. Your mother is tired of worrying that you will wind up dead in a ditch or behind a bar somewhere. Your brothers and sister are tired of your abuse, to them and to their friends. They can't bring their friends home because of you. And I can't do your dirty work anymore." Dad fixed me with a look of determination that I had never seen on his face before. "Nobody wants you here, Frank."

I don't recall making any response. I do remember, however, the rest of his words:

"We don't know what your problem is. I hope you identify and solve it. But you'll have to do it without us."

I may have asked where I should go. I don't remember. Anyway, Dad's decision that I should leave came with an offer. To his credit, and my gratitude, he was not evicting me without any concern for my well-being. He had an offer for me. He had arranged for me to be employed selling paint in Toronto. I knew a little about the paint business, though I knew next to nothing about Toronto.

He pressed a few dollars into my hand. It would be best, he said, if I left as soon as possible. He was right. I needed that job to make payments on my car. The next morning, I threw a few belongings in the back seat and headed west. No one waved goodbye.

[THREE]

Life on the Street

I drove along Highway 401 toward Toronto not in sorrow but in hope, spiked with a jigger of determination. I saw this as my chance to explore the side of me that I always knew existed, the one that I believed made me different from others, the one I could use to create some sort of life in place of the chaos I had been experiencing. I would exploit all those talents I believed were within me, whatever they might be. I would show my father and everyone else that I could achieve something in life after all.

Of course, it was all bravado. This time, I realized, I was on my own. This time there would be no one to pay the cabbie who drove me home, bail me out of jail, or see that I had food to eat and a roof over my head.

In Toronto I found a small apartment, started my job, and grew acquainted with the city. Meanwhile, my determination to succeed actually strengthened.

Toronto in 1970 had yet to become the multicultural dynamo it is today. Back then, the city lacked both the energy and the culture that defines it, to some of its citizens, as The Centre of the Universe. Montreal remained the source of Canadian joie de vivre. It was easy to find excitement in Montreal, and almost impossible to find a bad meal. In Montreal, the fashions were trendier, the music was livelier, the women were prettier, and the laughter was louder and more frequent. It took the FLQ crisis of October 1970 to send businesses scurrying west, following the route I had taken, and shift the economic centre of gravity to Toronto.

The transformation was beginning when I arrived, but Toronto remained mired in WASP tradition. The ultimate night out in Hogtown, as it was widely referred to in those days, still consisted of roast beef at the Royal York Hotel followed by a Mozart concert at Massey Hall. Eaton's department store dominated Yonge Street, although it was foolish to window-shop there on Sunday afternoons because the window displays were hidden behind heavy black curtains. Sundays in Toronto were not for something as frivolous as sports and shopping; they were for church-going. Drinking and carousing were suspected of being imported from Montreal, drifting down the 401 to arrive in Good Grey Toronto unbidden and unwelcome. To most people in Ontario, Montreal was a superficial town; Toronto was a Serious City.

The city's strait-laced demeanour may have influenced even me a little. I actually remained sober for a time, determined to prove my family wrong. It was not easy, especially at the beginning, when

I realized that much of my self-confidence was based on alcohol. The realization added to my desperate need for a drink, a need that I somehow managed to subdue. During my first few sales calls, I sat in my car steeling my nerve to walk in and try to sell something to someone I had never met before. I had some confidence in my ability to charm people, but I feared rejection as a salesman. If they didn't buy my paint, didn't that mean they hadn't been impressed with my sales ability? And if I hadn't impressed them, didn't that mean I was a failure?

In fact, I wasn't. Most of my customers liked me, they liked my sales pitch, and they liked the product I was selling. Over those first few weeks, I managed to impress the paint company and myself by scoring an impressive volume of sales. Every sale brought new confidence. I called on paint stores in communities west of Toronto and south into the Niagara region, many of them small towns where the Protestant work ethic was as much a part of the town as the war memorial in the park and the inevitable Chinese restaurant. At the end of each day, I prepared a call report identifying the paint dealers and hardware stores I had visited, and any sales I had made.

I became convinced that I would show them—"them" being my father in particular and the rest of the world in general—that I was as competent as anyone in the paint industry. I made many sales and several friends in those first few weeks. I paid my bills, took care of my health, and waited for the spirit of William Zeckendorf to nudge me toward some ultimate triumph. And from time to time, I had a drink or two. It felt good to drop into a bar after work. Or sometimes even during work—hey, you never knew when you might bump into a customer there.

Inevitably, the times between the drinks grew shorter and the time spent trading stories in bars grew longer.

One of my customers was an old friend of my father's named Bill Orr, who operated a paint and decorating store in Oakville, Ontario, about thirty kilometres west of Toronto. Bill and I hit it off immediately, not because of my father's connection or even because Bill was a knowledgeable and successful paint dealer—which he was—but because both of us liked to drink. The first time I called on Bill, we extended my sales presentation through a liquid lunch and well beyond. After that, I visited him as frequently as I could, because each visit ended at a bar, where I persuaded myself I was doing my job, trading stories with Bill, and taking turns picking up the tab.

I don't know what I might have done to impress Bill Orr as a paint salesman, but apparently he was impressed by my ability to consume alcohol. According to Bill, at my peak (if that's the term) I was drinking a forty-ounce bottle of whisky each day, day after day. I'll have to take his word for it.

After a month or two, I began skipping calls on customers: they were interfering with the time I could spend in the bar. Instead I sat drinking and forging call reports to make it look as if I was on the job. Predictably, my sales plummeted. Dealers began complaining that I hadn't visited them, despite what my call reports said, or that I had messed up their paint orders. My boss, who owned the company, was a nice fellow named Phil Chambers. Phil began warning me to pull up my socks and get back to working the way I had during those first few weeks on the job. Sometimes I did—for a while. Eventually, I began to ignore him.

One day I dropped in to see Bill Orr, who told me that Phil had called that morning. "He wants to talk to you," Bill said. "Apparently it's important. You should call him right away. You can use my phone if you want to."

I couldn't. I knew what the message would be. Phil was going to fire me, and I didn't have the nerve to make the call. Later, Phil had Bill Orr tell me himself. My sales career had lasted about four months.

Was I crushed or disappointed? No, I was neither. My only reaction was relief. Now I didn't have to lie anymore. I didn't have to make up stories and feel badly about disappointing a nice guy like Phil. Besides, I assured myself, I'd find another job soon. Until then, I was free to celebrate with a few drinks.

Losing my job triggered a chain of losses, each leading to the next, and for a time I felt as though I were riding an avalanche down the side of the mountain with neither the will nor the ability to stop it. The first—aside from my self-esteem and dreams of success, of course—was my car, repossessed because I hadn't made the loan payments. That wasn't so bad, I thought. Who needed a car when there were so many bars within a short walk of my apartment? I began haunting neighbourhood hangouts like the Silver Dollar, where the interior was dark and friendly, the drinks were cheap, and there was always someone to share a story or two.

Soon my landlord began complaining about unpaid rent. Tomorrow, I told him, I would start a new job and earn the rent I owed him. I told myself the same thing.

One evening, I stumbled home to find my few possessions stuffed into paper shopping bags and sitting outside my apartment door. The locks had been changed. The reaction of most people to discovering they had neither home nor job would be panic, I suppose. Mine was little more than a shrug, perhaps because I had expected it to happen, and because my sole priority once again was my next drink. I carried my possessions down to Union Station, the city's train station, and stuffed them into a rental locker. Then I went looking for a bottle of wine. The going price was ninety-nine cents for twenty-six ounces of barely drinkable sherry. The taste was terrible, but the effect was heavenly. When both the wine and my money were gone, I launched an extended search in pursuit of both.

I was, of course, responding emotionally, not logically, to my situation. Anyone could see that I was tumbling out of control into disaster. But one of the great lessons of life that I have learned is that few emotions are pure. We may love unconditionally, but other emotions are involved in our feelings, including fear of loss and rejection, and even a little resentment at the power over our happiness the other person has. When I laughed at losing my job, shrugged at losing my car, and walked away with everything I owned stuffed in paper bags and no place to sleep that night, my emotions were as mixed as ever. I felt indifference at my plight and even relief that someone else had made the decision that freed me to indulge in drinking full time. Merged with them were other feelings. Like humiliation, embarrassment, shame, and a good measure of self-loathing.

Back then, of course, I was successful at fooling myself. With park benches to sleep on and soft-hearted passers-by willing to drop a quarter into my outstretched palm, I figured things

weren't so bad. The biggest problems I faced were police officers and store owners who drove me away from the city's main
shopping areas. To avoid them, I wandered east to Jarvis Street.
Every city has its skid row, and Lower Jarvis Street was
Toronto's.

While panhandlers were more tolerated on Jarvis Street than
elsewhere, things weren't much easier. Street people were rarer
in the 1970s than they are today. If you were down and out, it had
to be your own damn fault. I was told, in several languages and
with various inflections, to "Get a job!" and it often took the
better part of a day to gather ninety-nine cents in a paper cup or
a trembling hand before the wine store closed.

Some of the Toronto police officers I encountered on skid
row were as malicious as anywhere else in the city. The decent
cops called through their patrol car window, "Come on, buddy,
move it along now," and I would trudge down the street to a
new spot. The nasty cops would leap from their cruiser as
though responding to a bank robbery. Slapping the cup out of
my hand and sending the coins flying, they snarled, "Move
your ass or I'll put the cuffs on you!" and glared at me as I
shuffled away, or followed me in the cruiser to make sure I left
the neighbourhood. When it appeared safe to return to my old
panhandling spot, I would search desperately for the coins
I had been accumulating all morning, getting down on my
hands and knees among the trash in the gutter and crawling
under parked cars to retrieve the precious nickels and dimes,
beyond humiliation.

If it hadn't been for Izzy Reingewertz, I would not have
survived those first few weeks on the street. Izzy is one of the

great figures in my life experience, a man who taught me a special lesson, not by preaching but by example. The lesson was this: Never give up on anyone.

I met Izzy during my early, productive, days of selling paint. He owned Exclusive Paints, a store at the corner of College and Spadina streets in downtown Toronto. This was not one of the city's classier intersections, and still isn't. In fact, the only thing "exclusive" about Izzy's store was the name on the sign. The place was crowded, dusty, and laid out like a rabbit warren. None of this mattered to Izzy's customers. They were attracted by the low prices. They also enjoyed hearing what Izzy had to say about paint, wallpaper, world politics, and life itself. Short and overweight, with a head of unruly white hair, Izzy could have been a character from a Broadway play. He and his wife, Ruth, treated their customers like extended family, cajoling, joking, bickering, and doling out free, often unsolicited, advice.

In many ways, Izzy was the Polish-Jewish equivalent of the French-Canadian Lemieux family. To suppliers who were being unfair or difficult, Izzy would shout and slap his fist on the counter, demanding lower prices, better payment terms, faster delivery, and often all three. To his friends and customers, who were often the same people, he would shake his head and mutter words of empathy and encouragement at their stories of hardship and difficulty, sometimes slipping a dollar or two into their hands.

Izzy's style may have been disconcerting to Toronto's WASP establishment, who preferred to buy their paint from clean, well-organized department stores, but it was a magnet for the influx of immigrants to the city. Mingled with Izzy's commentary on paint and politics were conversations in Croatian, Italian, Polish, Russian, Chinese, and a dozen other languages. Spending an hour in Izzy's store was like soaking up the ambience of the UN General Assembly on a day that the interpreters failed to show up. Izzy spread his rough-edged warmth on me from the first day I called on him as a paint salesman, and he kept dispensing it after it was obvious that my sales career had about as much future as a worn-out paint brush.

I remembered Izzy's generosity and understanding from my short-lived period of employment, and so, one morning when no one on Jarvis Street wanted to place a nickel in my hand, I walked across town to his store. There, behind a floor display of paint cans, I found Izzy and bluntly asked him for money. I think I called it a loan, but we both knew what it was.

Izzy studied me in silence for a moment before suggesting a better idea. "I won't give you a handout," he said. "But if you help me here in the store until noon, I'll pay you five dollars and I'll buy you lunch."

We had a deal. For the rest of the morning I swept the floor, carried paint up from the cellar, washed the windows, did whatever Izzy needed done. Then he took me to lunch, listened to my tale of woe, and, as we left the restaurant, pressed a five-dollar bill into my hand.

When things grew desperate enough over the next few months, and if I had the energy to hike it that far, I did chores around Izzy's store, and he would pay me five dollars. He set no quota on time or energy. I could work an hour before calling it quits or stay all morning. The reward was the same—a bowl of soup and a five-dollar bill to pay for a bottle or two of wine and a flophouse bed for the night.

Izzy's generosity was a godsend, but both he and I knew it had to be sporadic. He didn't need my labour more than twice a month, and I couldn't drag myself all the way to his store more often than that anyway. My primary source of cash remained the street, with its dangers and disgrace. I would stand with my hand out and my eyes cast downward, silently imploring those who passed to recognize me as a human being and to care enough to help me. Some did. Most didn't.

When the street proved unproductive, I resorted to more hazardous tactics. If I appeared presentable enough, I might enter a bar on Dundas or College Street, where I slid onto a stool and ordered first one beer and then another, running a tab as long as I dared. Then I took a slow, unsteady stroll to the washroom, followed by a brisk exit out the nearest door when the bartender's back was turned. This could work only once in each bar. Sometimes it failed to work at all. Nabbed by a suspicious bouncer before I could make my escape, it meant a punch to the head and a few kicks targeted at my ribs or crotch, along with a warning not to show my face there again.

If the opportunity presented itself, I might try the bold tactic of slipping the tip another patron had left for the bartender into my pocket. When the bartender complained about being stiffed by a cheap customer, I smiled and sympathized with him, sitting there with enough money to cover the beer I was drinking, and maybe another one as well. This device proved even riskier than skipping out without paying; stiffing the bar for a few drinks was bad enough, but stealing money from the bartender was inexcusable. Bouncers developed a sense of who might attempt this ploy, and they kept their eyes peeled for it. After palming forty or fifty cents off the bar, I would hear someone behind me mutter, "You son of a bitch!" as a beefy hand grabbed my neck or arm and tossed me out the door and into the street. If I encountered an especially angry bouncer, it resulted in a beating behind the bar, me crawling away with a bloody mouth and cracked ribs, facing a sleepless, painful night.

Spending nights on a park bench had turned out to be both uncomfortable and dangerous, but I often resorted to it out of sheer necessity. A night in the open air, if it were warm enough, meant fifty cents to spend on a bottle of wine instead of a flophouse bed. But summer nights also brought the risk of being pummelled by thugs who haunted the parks looking for someone to batter and kick, for victims without the strength, physically or emotionally, to fight back. No matter how much I fought back and asked my attackers to leave me alone, to find someone else, they never did. Not until they grew tired or bored. When the thugs finally left, I would drag myself back onto the bench again or, if I feared they would return, crawl along the ground to cower in the safety of bushes. If the pain was bad enough or the wounds wouldn't stop bleeding, I might find my way to a hospital or clinic to be patched up before returning to the street.

I don't know what drives young urban males to dish out the kind of abuse I suffered as a street person. Is the combination of excessive testosterone and the herd mentality really that powerful? Are youths of a certain stripe so angry that they can beat a helpless man until he is moaning and bleeding on the ground?

Sometimes the violence at least had a motive, as when thugs attacked me looking for money, taking whatever they could shake out of my hand or my pockets. Whether they found money or not, they usually delivered a punch or a kick before taking off.

To escape that pain and humiliation, I sometimes sought a bed in the Salvation Army hostel or the Fred Victor Mission. The mission had been built by a founding member of the immensely wealthy Massey family and named for Hart Massey's son, who died tragically young. I have always found it interesting that the Masseys made their impact on both ends of Toronto society, providing penniless derelicts with beds and hot meals at the Fred Victor Mission, and presenting the upper strata with Massey Hall, a venue for cultural and social exposure.

Most of us avoided the hostel and the mission when we could. We rebelled against the gospel lessons of the Salvation Army and the rigid rules at the Fred Victor. We preferred to spend fifty cents a night for a shared flophouse room, where you tied your shoelaces around your ankles before you fell asleep because, if your shoes were in better shape than those of your roommates, you would wake in the morning to find your companions—and your shoes—gone.

The sheets weren't clean and the rooms weren't warm, but the flophouses were free of rules, and that made a difference. Others may have considered us bums and hopeless alcoholics, but we saw ourselves as free spirits, liberated from the cares of the people who went home every night to families and soft beds. The straight people, the ones with jobs and families, may have been comfortable but, we told ourselves, they paid a price for that comfort. They were bound to the expectations of others, prisoners of their own needs and ambition. We had no expectations of ourselves, and no one had any of us. We were free—free to beg, free to drink, free to make plans for the future if we chose to. Why should we trade our freedom for a warm room, clean sheets, regular meals, and a steady income?

Of course, something was missing from that picture. We were free to starve and be beaten and murdered as well. Free to be insulted and belittled. Free to cry alone.

We watched other people walk or drive past, pretending they weren't seeing us, pretending they were lost in their own concerns, their own worries. We knew better. What did they have to worry about that was so important? Did they worry about being a nickel short or arriving a minute too late at the wine store? Perhaps they thought we had nothing to worry about because we lacked a car to maintain, a house to pay for, a family to raise. Perhaps they believed we were the free ones. If so, they were wrong. Do not believe that myth about street people enjoying their freedom, that they secretly sing *Hallelujah, I'm a bum!* while standing with outstretched palms asking for spare coins. With the exception of seriously mentally ill people, those who live on the streets of our cities *want* to change, they *want* to escape the dirt and find the way out. There is nothing exhilarating about standing in the street on a cold, rainy day in Toronto or Saskatoon or Edmonton or Halifax or anywhere. There is no glamour to shivering in the cold, no charm to a perpetually empty stomach, and there is certainly no reward to being "free" under those conditions.

At times when I acknowledged the other side of my so-called freedom, I sought out a dark corner in a back alley, away from my companions and the thugs in the park. There I huddled against the side of a building and cried, repeating over and over "tomorrow … tomorrow … tomorrow" until I fell asleep. Tomorrow I'll stop drinking. Tomorrow I'll get a job and become a great salesman again. Tomorrow I'll talk to my parents. Tomorrow, tomorrow.

Some people harbour a romantic notion of brotherhood among men who lived as I was living, imagining that we looked out for each other, cared about each other, protected each other. Unfortunately, it's mostly fiction. A kind of fraternal relationship might exist in the morning, when the day stretched before us and we were confident of begging the ninety-nine cents for wine, plus fifty cents for a room, and perhaps an extra quarter or two for coffee. But as the day unfolded and our hands and cups remained empty, it became every man for himself.

Even if it was a good day of panhandling, I concealed my money from Doc and Bruce and the others, men whose company I had shared so easily when the day began, out of fear that they would overpower me and leave me penniless with no hope of begging another dollar before the wine store closed. The jokes, stories, and laughter faded with the light, except on those rare days when we had all been successful, scoring a few dollars each, grinning as we counted the coins on our way to the wine store. Then we were friends again, each with his bottle, drifting side by side on separate hazy streams. But these were rare and treasured times. Usually I lived in my own head, in my own space, with my own thoughts and nightmares.

One of the benefits of drinking was that it enabled me to be anyone and anything I wanted to be. When drunk, I boasted that I had been the world's greatest salesman until betrayed by ungrateful customers and incompetent managers. I bragged about being a friend of Pierre Trudeau. I claimed that I could call him on the telephone any time I chose, because Trudeau knew my name; Trudeau was an old buddy of my father, who happened to be one of the wealthiest men in Canada; Trudeau would give me a job if I asked for one. There was always a germ of truth within my tales. I had, after all, worked on Trudeau's election campaign, and my father *was* a businessman, wealthy by the standards of the street.

My friends spun their stories as well, and I learned to recognize the basic truths supporting the layers of lies. Bruce really had been a businessman, I discovered, though I suspected that his tale of losing all of his hard-earned assets after being deceived by his partners wasn't true. The only deception had been his own, when he chose the bottle over family, friends, and business. Stan refused to discuss his past, but Doc really had been a physician, a bona fide doctor who lost his licence because of his alcoholism. He also lost his family, who gave up on him, and, inevitably, somewhere along the line he lost his self-respect. Doc had been brilliant and ambitious enough to succeed in medical school, but he failed at life. His failure no longer mattered because nobody really cared what he had done in the past. Each of us could have come from royalty or from squalor. The origins made no difference in the way we assessed each other. Our stories served as entertainment, not education.

Doc was just another grizzled drunk on Jarvis Street, worth tossing a quarter at and nothing more. On a couple of occasions,

Doc claimed, he recognized passers-by as former patients. "I remember that guy," he would whisper, pointing at a man who had just passed us, keeping his eyes averted and his hands in his pockets. "I treated him for kidney stones."

His patients never recognized Doc, of course, not only because he no longer wore a starched white smock and a stethoscope, but because street people are essentially faceless. Most people cannot dredge from memory the face of the most recent person to ask them for spare change. Beggars are faceless, not only to passers-by but to their former colleagues. I remember much about the tales Joe and Bruce and Doc and others told me, about the good life they once enjoyed and their reasons for being down and out. But I cannot recall their faces. Everything about them fades to grey; nothing remains of their individuality beyond a few facts reluctantly shared. They become grey people, grey in their total lack of differentiation, grey in their anonymity. Among the many ways that street life is dehumanizing, this remains perhaps the most telling.

Whenever I describe this period of my life to people today, I see the question forming in their eyes, and soon they express it aloud: *What was it really like, living that way?* It is impossible to describe; it is not a place so much as a state of being, an absence of everything but hope, and even then, very little of that.

The only word I could use to describe it is *dirty*. Everything on the street is dirty. The gutters are dirty, you're dirty, your clothes are dirty, and your friends are dirty. If you manage to score a bed in a flophouse for the night, the mattress is dirty. If you choose to sleep on the floor, well, that's dirty too. You cannot escape the dirt. Life on the street is like eating off a dirty plate. You rub the dirt off one spot, so you can have just one small patch of cleanliness, but as soon as you stop rubbing, the dirt returns and starts shrinking the shiny area you worked so hard to clean. As much as I might try to rub that spot clean, the dirt encroached, the clean part vanishing, until I felt like giving up. I couldn't win. The dirt would win. The dirt always won. And to some of us, the dirt no longer mattered. We stopped worrying about it. There was so much, after all, to worry about already.

After about six months on the street, I began accepting the fact that I was doomed if I did not change my life. At first, the idea was easy to ignore. If I had a bottle of wine all to myself and a flophouse room waiting, and if the weather was mild and my friends remained my friends, what did it matter? I would enjoy today. But as time passed, the idea niggled more and more, until it became difficult to shut out even with drink.

If I had experienced a moment of epiphany or some golden sunbeam signifying the finger of God reaching down to flick sense into me, my story would be more dramatic but less instructive. There was neither. I simply recall a mounting awareness that the life I was living ran counter to every value my father, my teachers, and my church had taught me, counter to all the lessons I had absorbed from good people like the Lemieuxs.

Many of those values were based on a firm foundation of trust. My values had no foundation, if I even claimed to have any. This realization that I was living my life in contradiction of every core value in my being launched my journey off the street. I did not change my life after waking up drenched with my own vomit in a jail cell, or lying in a fetal position with a gang of creeps kicking my ribs for the sheer joy of it. One way or another, I had endured those kinds of things for years. Instead, it was the burrowing awareness that Frank O'Dea, who had been taught decent values as a youngster, could no longer be trusted. He would die not being trusted or cared about. He would die alone and unmissed, and he would die soon. Unless …

I didn't care what or who had turned a basically good kid from Montreal West into a drunk on Jarvis Street. Nothing could be gained by blaming my plight on my distant parents or voluptuous Lana or Murphy the cop or the predatory priests. My guilt and my shame could not be passed along to others like a hot potato, or washed away in a shower stall. They were mine, and it was my duty to dispose of them.

I had been repeating "tomorrow, tomorrow …" over the years.

Tomorrow finally arrived two days before Christmas.

DECEMBER 23, 1971, was a Thursday. In Toronto, the day began cloudy and mild, with the temperature rising to just above zero Celsius. It would turn colder later in the day. Snow flurries were expected overnight. The skies would clear Friday and the weekend would be sunny. The temperature would continue to drop. Christmas Day would be clear and frigid.

I'm not describing the weather from memory. I looked it up at the library. I recall nothing about the weather forecast for that day. I hadn't read or listened to one for months. I remember only that I rose on the morning of December 23 before Doc and Bruce. While they continued sleeping, I walked out of the shelter wearing the same dirty blue jeans, stained T-shirt, and worn plaid shirt that had once been blue but was now faded into a bilious shade of green.

I was feeling positive when I woke, even jubilant. It would be a good day for panhandling. People feel generous at Christmastime. They respond with concern to guys like me, shivering in torn jeans and dirty shirt, shuffling along the sidewalk with extended hand and downcast eyes. I might get all the cash I needed by noon and have the rest of the day to stay mellow.

I tottered out the door and across the street to the small park at the corner of Jarvis and Shuter, where I stood shivering in the cold air. I would wait there for Doc and Bruce and Stan and the others to emerge, with the same sleepy and somewhat bewildered expression I was wearing, to plan our strategy for the day. The goal was always the same: to cadge ninety-nine cents for a bottle of wine and fifty cents for another night in the shelter. Those were the boundaries of our lives. Only the execution varied. Would we beg for money on Dundas Street, or venture to Yonge Street, where the traffic was heavier but the risk of being accosted by the police higher? Would we search for discarded bottles in alleys and earn a few pennies in deposit refunds? Would we even survive another day on the street? The question of survival had been bothering me for some time. Now, standing alone in the morning chill, I began to focus on it.

With my hands in my pockets, my body trembling, my stomach tossing, and my mind racing, I shuffled through the hard facts: Unless I changed my life, I would die like this. I would die alone, and I would die soon. Anyone who had watched me stumble from tree to telephone pole, clutching each as a means of remaining on my feet, or who had turned their heads from the sight of me bloodied from a beating or wearing the contents of my stomach on my clothing, knew that I could not continue living as I had been. I knew it as well as they did. Others recognized this reality in a heartbeat. It had taken me thirteen years.

Again, I don't wish to embellish the moment I realized and accepted the fact. As I have admitted, no sunbeam parted the clouds to shine upon me. I heard no encouraging voice or rousing choruses of inspirational music. Visions of angels or spirits didn't appear before me, and no acquired words of wisdom rose up from my memory. I know only that the realization settled on me like a physical weight: *If I don't change, I will die like this.*

I hadn't had a pressing need to change my life for years. No motivation or incentive. No promise or assurance. No epiphany or intellectual analysis. I had only that momentary, even fleeting, acceptance of an existing truth, accompanied by the hope that I could finally do what I had always known I must do. I did not want to die on the street.

The wind came up, pulling at my shirt. I turned my back on it and stepped closer to a tree for shelter, facing Jarvis Street. A car passed, driven by an attractive woman. The back seat was piled with Christmas gifts. I looked up at the apartments on Jarvis Street and saw Christmas decorations in the windows. A billboard on the corner showed an impossibly cheerful Santa

Claus waving at two perfect children. Somewhere a radio began playing carols, and in the midst of it all I said it again, this time aloud: *If I don't change, I am going to die like this.* And I added, silently: *Today, tomorrow, the next day, whenever. I will die alone and shivering, just as I am now. When I do, few will know I am gone, and even fewer will care.*

Those were the only options left: Die or change.

I remembered something then, something about people who would help get me off the street. It was a radio commercial I had heard on one of those mornings working at Izzy's. I recalled nothing about the advertisement except that it promoted a self-help group, and that its tag line was: *If you have a problem with alcohol, call us. We're in the book.*

I stepped out of the park onto the sidewalk and began begging for money. I had never done this alone, never before Doc and the others woke and joined me. This time was different. This time, all I wanted was a dime. When I managed to get one, I walked to a telephone booth on the corner and looked up the organization's number. "I need to talk to somebody," I told whoever answered. I don't remember if it was a man or a woman. I just remember my words, and the desperation in them. The voice on the other end invited me to come right over. The Yonge Street address was not far from where I was standing. I turned my back on the flophouse and began walking.

The offices were on the second floor of a nondescript building that has long since been demolished. I managed to climb the stairs, pulling myself hand over hand on the banister, feeling as bedraggled as I looked, unwashed, unshaven, and wearing everything I owned on my back.

I paused at the top of the stairs to regain my breath and rebuild my determination. Then I turned the corner. Facing me was a woman with white hair and glasses, seated behind a small, cluttered desk. I could think of nothing to say except, "I need help."

The woman broke into a radiant smile and said: "You're home."

[FOUR]

Good Decisions, Bad Decisions

Marg Meek proved as welcoming and gracious as her smile. She shook my hand, poured me a mug of coffee, and handed me a pamphlet to read. The pamphlet looked familiar, and I realized it was the same one my Northern Electric buddies and I had laughed at in a bar a few years earlier. This time, of course, it wasn't so amusing.

I remained there all day, sipping coffee, reading magazines, chatting with Marg, and staying warm. Soon after five o'clock, a new shift of volunteers arrived. Among them was a well-groomed Bay Street investment executive named Joe, who invited me to join him for dinner across the street at Basel's Restaurant.

While Joe had never been a street person like me, he had almost lost everything of value to him—his family, his career, and his self-respect—from the same addiction that was killing me.

I panhandled for wine; Joe had snuck out for martinis. I got drunk in alleys; Joe had gotten drunk in nightclubs, in his office, and at home. My clothes came from Goodwill; his had come from Holt Renfrew. The one thing that connected us was alcohol and our determination to beat it.

The guidance Joe gave me that evening was blunt and direct: Forget about the mistakes you made yesterday; yesterday is gone. Don't dwell on tomorrow; nobody knows what it will bring. Focus exclusively on today. When you wallow in remorse over yesterday, or quake in fear about tomorrow, you lose hope.

When I heard those words, I realized hope was all I had.

"You don't need to take life even one day at a time, if that's too much," Joe advised me. "Take it an hour at a time. A minute at a time, if you can stay off alcohol that way." He handed me a fistful of dimes and a telephone number scribbled on a slip of paper. "Use the dimes to call me from a pay phone when you feel the need for a drink, when you think you can't stand not drinking anymore. Any time you have a craving for a drink, you call me. Understand?" He had a no-nonsense attitude. Having gone through the same thing as I had, he knew the temptation to backslide, and all the ways I might fool myself.

I told him I understood. I promised I would not let him down.

"It's not me you should worry about letting down," Joe said. "It's yourself."

I opened my hand and studied the dimes. A day ago that much money would have sent me off to the wine store with a grin and a rapidly building thirst. The very gesture of handing me the coins had been an expression of trust. Someone was trusting me again.

"Where are you sleeping tonight?" Joe asked.

I told him I didn't know.

"Where do you sleep when you have the money?"

I named the flophouse on Jarvis Street.

He handed me fifty cents to cover the room charge. "It'll be tempting," he said. "Just remember that. It'll be tempting to have a drink with your buddies—just one, you'll tell yourself. If you do, you'll be right back where you started." As we said goodbye outside the restaurant, Joe shook my hand. "The next few weeks are going to be difficult," he said. "But you know what? The hardest part is already over."

I headed back to Jarvis Street, paid for my room, tied my shoelaces around my ankles, and fell onto a cot. For the first time in years, I fell asleep in a state of total sobriety. When I woke the next morning, my first thought was to get my hands on a bottle of wine. My second thought was to call Joe.

"You have a drink last night?" Joe asked over the phone.

I told him truthfully that I hadn't.

"Good," Joe said. "If you feel like having one today, call me first. Don't forget."

In many ways, I was fortunate—fortunate in remembering the radio commercial I had heard at Izzy's, fortunate in having someone as supportive as Joe to guide me, and fortunate in not experiencing severe withdrawal symptoms when I gave up drinking. The craving remained, however, and I used my entire supply of dimes that day calling Joe to say how much I wanted a drink.

"You called me, and that's good," Joe said. "It means your desire to stop is stronger than your urge to have another drink. You're strong. You can do it." I wasn't sure I believed him.

That evening when we met, he gave me another handful of dimes. He wished me a Merry Christmas—it was Christmas Eve, after all.

The next day was my first Christmas away from home. I had spoken to no one in my family for months. My father knew my career as a paint salesman had ended long ago. Did he and my mother have any idea where I was? Did they know if I was dead or alive? Did they care? I considered calling them, just to hear them wish me a Merry Christmas and express their concern for me. I wasn't certain that they would, of course. If I didn't, I feared my remorse would be too much to handle without alcohol. Besides, I had not solved my problem yet. I would not call them until I had.

For Christmas dinner, I visited the Fred Victor Mission, where I and a few hundred others stood in line to be served roast turkey with all the trimmings: mashed potatoes, bread stuffing, cranberry sauce, giblet gravy, plum pudding, coffee—everything but wine. Among the servers were politicians and celebrities. The food was delicious, and when the plates were cleared, everyone was invited to join in singing Christmas carols.

It sounds like a merry place to be on Christmas Day, but it wasn't. You cannot forget years of desperation and futility overnight. You cannot ask people whose quality of life depends on a few coins in their hand or dregs in a wine bottle to overflow with joy and happiness at the drop of a hat. The most pleasant part of Christmas is sharing the season with family and friends. I was seated among strangers, though some faces appeared familiar. My memory of the past few months was hardly reliable. Perhaps they had been friends on the street. Perhaps not.

As the carol singing began, I realized I had been sober for two days. I had not been sober for two consecutive days since high school.

Those of us seated at the same table that evening knew little of each other, and we could not have cared less. We were together only because no one else would have us, and we were dining together because we had nowhere else to go. All of us knew and accepted that. So we ate quietly for the most part, thankful for the meal. When the carol singing began, it was aimless and half-hearted, not a song of joy but merely payment for a full belly.

In the middle of the singing I rose from my chair and shuffled toward the washroom. Locking the door behind me, I leaned against the wall and cried like a lost child.

I FOLLOWED A DIFFICULT ROUTINE for about three weeks. My nights were still spent in a Jarvis Street flophouse, avoiding guys I had known for so long and trying to sleep without a drink. My days were spent wandering through shopping malls and department stores, anywhere I could keep warm and dry and close to a telephone, should the temptation to enter a bar begin worming its way through my mind. When this happened, I called Joe or one of the other volunteers who had given me their telephone numbers, and they would remind me to take one minute at a time if I had to. I must stay sober.

Each day I ran through my supply of dimes, making sure to save at least one to call Joe at five o'clock. Each evening, he and I met with others, usually in a church basement. These were people like me and like the man Joe had been. We told of our experiences. We offered support. We mourned the absence of those who had attended these meetings in their attempt to give up alcohol and had failed.

After each meeting, we walked to a nearby restaurant for sandwiches and coffee. I was about as acquainted with members of this group as I had been with those Christmas Day diners at the mission, yet we shared a genuine feeling of companionship that had been missing from the Christmas celebration. Unlike the stories I had heard from my street companions, the ones we traded in our meetings were tales of hope and achievement, recollections of how this man had licked his addiction, how that woman had overcome her constant craving, how somebody else was now sober and married and holding down a steady job. These people no longer talked about "tomorrow" because they were busy living and enjoying today.

Each storyteller had a unique tale of success and failure. But it wasn't important that their circumstances weren't exactly like mine. The important point was that somebody had achieved the same goal I had set for myself. I wanted to hear how they succeeded and decide if the same technique could work for me. I was willing to try anything that made my goal more attainable.

I had one vision: to remain sober, one day at a time. If I could do that, I might realize the image of myself I had been harbouring since I was a boy, the one in which I became a reincarnated Zeckendorf, battling my way against all odds to achieve some ill-defined measure of success. I no longer wanted anything to do with "tomorrow." I wanted to start today.

Let me make one thing clear: This was no smooth, continuous journey; no elevator ride from a cold, rat-infested basement to the penthouse. Over those first weeks, I often doubted my courage, my resolve to succeed. A dollar in my hand, I knew, could buy a bottle of wine. With that and a park bench, I could enjoy a mindless afternoon, free from pain and fears of the future.

Fear had been the most prevalent emotion in my life, and it was still with me. I felt fear at the sight of a uniformed police officer, remembering the cops' disgust at the sight of me on the street. I feared not being able to live up to the promise I had made Joe and myself, and I feared my past catching up to me. I still feared whatever lurked around the next corner, wherever that corner might be. Through this whole period, I felt as if I were carrying a football in my stomach, one that threatened to explode and send me back to Jarvis Street with Doc and Bruce and Stan, where at least the fear was more definable.

I was especially terrified that my new friends, whom I admired for their achievements, would discover the kind of person I had been and reject me. The thought panicked me. My family had rejected me, and I no longer could count on my buddies from the street, the only people who had placed a value on my existence in recent months. What if my new friends discovered the things I had done, the things I *had* to do to survive? Would they shake their heads in disgust and turn away? As irrational as this may seem now—after all, what did I know of the things *they* might have done in the darkest periods of their lives?—the fear was real and disturbing.

Fortunately, I revelled in a new emotion: excitement. I was excited at the possibilities my life was offering, possibilities that were barely conceivable just a few weeks earlier. Whenever the fear that I might succumb to another drink crept up on me, I drew on the excitement of succeeding. Whenever I felt as though I were sliding back, I remembered the feeling I had when Marg Meek said, "You're home"—the feeling of being out of the cold and in a warm place I never wanted to leave.

At the end of January, I was struck by an amazing insight. The realization stopped me in my tracks, there in the middle of a busy sidewalk. While other people flowed around me, I stood shaking my head and smiling, as though a pile of money lay at my feet, or I had just remembered the punch line of a joke.

I was going to make it. That was the realization. I had been sober for over a month, and *I would stay sober, one day at a time.* I knew this with the same certainty that I knew I was going to achieve something important. I was no longer relying on hope alone. Now I had some self-assurance. Not a lot of it, but enough to help me hold my head up and ignore most of my fears.

My self-confidence drew me closer to my new, sober, friends. We continued supporting each other, though not always with success. Over time, some found themselves unable to resist the lure of a drink. Whenever this happened, the rest of us refused to lose confidence in ourselves. In fact, the reverse occurred—we grew stronger, we drew closer together, we built up our resolve.

One evening, Joe pulled me aside and said, "Frank, it's time you got a job." I went with him to a used clothing store, where he had me fitted out with a suit, a couple of shirts, and a tie. Then he gave me some names to call. Within a few days I was selling industrial equipment to clean grime off buildings, statues, and production machines. With a loan from Joe against my first salary cheque, I rented a small basement apartment tucked behind a shopping centre. There was still nothing magical or glamorous about my life, but then, there had been nothing magical or glamorous about living on the street either.

Had Zeckendorf started this way? I doubted it, but I didn't care. I immersed myself in the details, practised my sales technique, kept myself well-groomed, and got started. Salesmanship is like riding a bicycle: Once you've mastered the technique, it stays with you. I visited prospects, listened closely to their needs, answered their questions, and closed the sale. Not all of them, of course. But enough to justify my salary.

After staying sober for almost a year, I found enough willpower to contact my family. It took an enormous amount of strength to lift the telephone receiver, dial the number, and wait for someone to answer the telephone.

If I expected Mom and Dad to express delight over my news, I was mistaken. They sounded encouraged to hear that I no longer drank, that I was successful at my job, and that I had lifted myself up by the bootstraps. But who could blame them for remaining skeptical? I had spent half my lifetime, after all, lying to them and everyone else, including myself. How could one telephone call erase all that? I believed in myself, but why should they?

Besides, the family had new concerns. Dad had left his job with the paint company to market premixed joint cement for use in drywall construction. He had developed the material, which he named ODO. The product was ahead of its time. Today, the same material is used in almost every construction project on the continent. But in business, as in everything else, timing is everything, and Dad's timing had not been good. The market was slow to respond, Dad's capital was too thin, and his company wound up in bankruptcy. The failure pained my father, I know, as much as anything that happened in his life. Including me.

AROUND THE TIME I PHONED MY FAMILY, I began dating Joanne, a petite blond woman I had met at one of the group sessions. Unlike others at the meeting, Joanne did not have a drinking problem. She attended to support a favourite uncle of hers who needed help with his alcohol addiction. We chatted easily the first evening we met. At the next session, I invited her for a coffee, then to dinner, and soon we were dating steadily.

I needed and welcomed the companionship, but I had been sober for less than a year, and I knew that many recovering alcoholics, even those as determined as me to stay sober, began to believe after several months that they were strong enough to have a social drink or two. I knew I would not drink again, but only if I kept drawing on my resolve, if I kept reminding myself of the promises I had made. I remained uncertain about many things—my prospects for a career, my connection with my family, and my sexuality. Still, Joanne and I had fun, and the seeds of a potential long-term relationship were planted. She was easy to talk to and had a positive outlook on life. I thrived on the attention she paid me.

I needed someone to accept me both for what I was and what I had been. She knew of my past, of course, and perhaps by dating me she fulfilled some personal need to care for someone, to help that person realize whatever potential she sensed in him. Joanne sensed potential in me.

We attended meetings of the self-help group together, we went to movies and concerts, and we laughed a lot—never underestimate the healing power of laughter.

After some time, Joanne grew so confident in our relationship that she persuaded me to visit her family in Montreal.

Joanne had discussed her parents only in the broadest of terms, explaining that her mother and father were divorced, and that we would be staying with her mother and stepfather. I had no idea of her family's wealth or social status until our cab from the airport stopped in front of an elegant Westmount mansion, and her mother emerged to greet us. Later, I met Joanne's father, who lived on Nuns' Island, near Montreal, with his wife. I found him somewhat aloof, a towering presence. He didn't reject or insult me, but he didn't go out of his way to make me feel at home either. This was due, I decided, at least as much to the tension between him and his ex-wife as to my questionable qualities as a prospective son-in-law.

At some point during our visit, I overheard Joanne and her mother discussing our relationship. Both parents seemed to consider our relationship permanent, and pleased that Joanne was prepared to settle down. Despite my background and my lack of social standing, Joanne's family accepted me. Marriage had never crossed my mind, but after a few days of sampling the family's wealth and rubbing elbows with Westmount society, the idea took hold. Wedding plans started being discussed. I was flattered and intrigued. Marriage? To a beautiful, intelligent woman from a prominent Westmount family? Well, why not? We returned to Toronto officially engaged.

When I told one of my support-group counsellors about the plans, he shook his head in disapproval. "Bad decision, Frank," he said. "We advise people who are getting over an addiction as severe as yours not to make any major plans for at least a full year."

"I'm not making any major plans," I answered. "I'm just getting married." It is a mark of my immaturity at the time, I suppose, that I said this without irony.

The event was everything expected of a Westmount wedding, though it led to a complicated post-ceremony reception. So much enmity remained between Joanne's parents that having them both attend the reception, smiling and posing as proud parents, was out of the question. We had two guest lists, two receptions, two wedding cakes, and two series of toasts to the bride and groom—one hosted by Joanne's mother and stepfather, the other by her father and stepmother.

My parents attended the wedding and reception hosted by Joanne's mother, and while they were as pleased as any parents would be to see their ne'er-do-well son marrying into Westmount society, they were also skeptical. Something was wrong here, they were thinking. Frank, the son from hell who stole and destroyed cars, who couldn't hold a job, and who alienated almost everyone he met, was about to enter the highest strata of society? It was too outlandish, too much of a Hollywood ending. Mom and Dad didn't think it would last.

Joanne and I honeymooned at her family's oceanfront villa in Kennebunkport, Maine, the same town favoured by U.S. president George H.W. Bush and his family. We spent a wonderful week watching storms roar off the Atlantic and waves crash against the rocky coast before returning to our stylish apartment in midtown Toronto, our wedding gifts waiting to furnish its several rooms. I returned to work selling equipment and Joanne began decorating the apartment with great style and flair.

In less than two years I had gone from being a skid row panhandler to a member of an influential Westmount family. I ate steak and placed my head on feather pillows each night. In the morning, I woke in a warm room next to a beautiful woman who received a monthly allowance from her wealthy family. I had everything I once longed for.

The marriage, of course, was a disaster.

Joanne and I married for vastly different reasons. I'm not sure what Joanne's motives were, other than a deep affection for me. My motives were based on the security and respect that marriage to Joanne provided. This has nothing to do with her being a sweet woman who cared for me, and whom I cared about as well. Barely a year earlier, getting my hands on a dollar bill before noon was all I needed to fulfill a day of my life. By marrying Joanne, I began living well. Standing at the altar, I wasn't holding the hand of my bride as much as the key to a fairy-tale future, or so I thought. Anyone who tries to build a marriage on that premise is a fool. I knew this at the time but I couldn't, or chose not to, resist it.

There were other factors besides my selfish motive. Still confused about my sexuality, I thought marriage to an attractive woman would finally define it to me and to the world. I was wrong, of course. To compound things, Joanne's personality at the time was not strong enough to deal with all the problems and insecurities I still carried with me. Joanne was fortunate that her life had been sheltered from darker aspects of the world. I envied her for that, but I soon realized that my experiences on Jarvis Street might as well have occurred on Mars when it came to explaining who I was, and who I had been for so long.

As much as we enjoyed each other's company, Joanne and I failed to connect as two people prepared to dedicate our lives to each other, and we slowly drifted apart, creating a gulf between us that none of our good intentions could bridge. She could not accept the person I once was, and I resented her inability to understand my experience. She wanted me to be more open about myself; I grew less and less communicative. She strived to be open; I insisted on being closed. Our disagreements produced angry words separated by long sullen silences. Eventually nothing between us worked. Nothing justified our being together.

The marriage lasted barely six months. It ended when Joanne returned to Westmount, phoning me from there to tell me it was over. Initially, I felt only relief. Once again, someone else had made a decision for me. Other emotions came later.

When I agreed we should separate, she insisted that I vacate the apartment before she returned from Montreal. While I looked for a place to live, Joanne's family sent her to Europe for rest, relaxation, and therapy to repair her shattered state. We were divorced sometime later.

Had I acted like a cad? Probably. Perhaps I should have heeded my counsellor's warnings. I beat myself up for a long time over the failure of our marriage, but life moves on. Besides, there's a warm ending to the tale.

More than twenty years after Joanne's parting telephone call, I was earning a good deal of local media exposure through my association with a high-profile charitable event. For several days, my face and name appeared in newspapers, I was interviewed on television, and I became something of a minor celebrity. Not long after the media attention faded, I received a letter. Joanne's name was on the return address.

A letter from an ex-spouse is not necessarily something you embrace with unbridled enthusiasm; it took me three days to find the nerve to open it and read its contents. I needn't have worried. Joanne's note congratulated me on my achievements and suggested we get together for coffee and a chat. A few days later, we met at a downtown restaurant.

Joanne appeared as attractive and vibrant as ever. She explained that her escape to Europe after the breakup of our marriage had led to an interest in psychotherapy. In fact, she became more than merely interested: she studied at some of the most prestigious institutes in the world, becoming a highly respected psychotherapist who works with abused women. Occasionally, she appears as a guest expert on radio and television shows dealing with marital relationships. The single mother of a lovely daughter, her life is both challenging and satisfying. I told Joanne how much I admired her for her achievements and how much she deserved the happiness she was obviously enjoying.

When we had finished our coffee, I offered to drive her home. Stepping out of my car, she paused for a moment, then turned back to me. "You know something, Frank?" she said. "I'm glad I married you."

I felt honoured by her words, and I drove home wearing a broad smile, bathed in a warm glow.

[FIVE]

Bulldozers, Coin Sorters, and Coffee

Every divorce is an admission of failure on both sides, and when Joanne and I separated, the risk that I might return to my dependence on alcohol was very real. But not to me. I suppose the fact that I rejected the end of our marriage as an excuse to resume drinking was a mark of my determination to remain sober, but my support group deserved at least as much credit. They encouraged openness and discussion about the most personal aspects of our lives, so it wasn't difficult to discuss my impending divorce and reveal that my soon-to-be-ex wife had insisted I leave our apartment. Where would I live?

Someone suggested I call a man named Peter Waters who lived in Oakville, Ontario. After overcoming his addiction problems,

Peter first launched a successful business, then entered politics, serving as a town councillor. Peter never forgot the aid he received from others, and he repaid the debt by opening his home to people like me. "We keep sober," Peter would say, "by helping other drunks." I was no longer a drunk, but his offer of a room was a godsend, and in 1973 I exchanged the non-stop hubbub of downtown Toronto for the restrained lifestyle of Oakville.

I suppose there are more conservative communities in Canada than Oakville, but I can't think of any. Through the 1970s and 1980s, the town boasted the highest median income in Canada. It also prided itself on being a community that resisted change. When neighbouring towns were embracing new housing developments and approving shopping centres within their boundaries, Oakville rejected both. As a result, its downtown core remained compact and vibrant, and the value of the impressive homes along the Lake Ontario shoreline grew to spectacular heights. Quiet, comfortable, and conservative, Oakville appeared an ideal place to prepare myself for whatever the next adventure might be.

Hope had held me together on Jarvis Street. A vision got me off it, and away from a life that would have soon killed me. Now I was taking action, making a foundation for a new life. *Hope. Vision. Action.* I wasn't conscious of it at the time, but much of my life from that point forward has been constructed on those three principles.

By THIS TIME, I had acquired a measure of self-confidence in some areas. Not arrogance—after the previous years of my life, I was in no danger of becoming arrogant about my success. I mean the self-confidence born of knowing you possess a certain innate talent in greater quantity than other people. In my case, the talent was salesmanship. I could talk to people easily and earn their trust. Most important, I could sense their needs and find a way to meet them with the product I was selling. Salesmanship, in its widest definition, is like a talent for music and art, and I made the best use of it. You can train and motivate a salesperson, but you cannot make one. Good salespeople bring a unique blend of talents to the job, and somewhere along the way I had acquired the aptitude of connecting with prospects and persuading them that my product was the ideal answer to their needs.

With the move to Oakville in 1973, I applied my sales abilities to heavy construction equipment. The job involved visiting building contractors and the heads of construction firms, to whom I promoted the benefits of tractors, backhoes, bulldozers, excavators, and other machinery that I had known nothing about just a few weeks earlier. Didn't matter. I had immersed myself in the things that these machines did better than others, and started making calls. I scored enough sales to assure my boss that he had made a good decision in hiring me.

The job provided both an income and a car, and within a couple of months I moved out of Peter's home and into my own apartment. Skid row remained close, geographically at least, and I made a point of driving down Jarvis Street from time to time. Whenever I saw someone I might have known from my life on the street, I pulled over to offer a word of encouragement and slip a dollar or two into his hand. Bruce was still there, still talking about tomorrow—tomorrow he would get a job, tomorrow he would stop drinking, tomorrow, tomorrow. No one had seen Stan in months and I didn't know if this was good or bad news. But everyone knew about Doc.

Doc, who had fallen farther than any of us, from licensed physician to street person, found a way of falling even farther by throwing himself off the Bloor Street Viaduct, dropping a hundred feet into the valley below. There would be no tomorrow for Doc.

But there *would* be a tomorrow for me, and it would be better than today. Having transformed hope into a vision, I was now taking action.

One day, while chatting with Joe Green, one of the other construction-equipment salesmen, I told him about once bragging to my mother that I would have a million dollars by the time I was thirty-five. It was the kind of thing young men toss out all the time. Someday I'll be sales manager. Someday I'll go to Hawaii. Someday I'll have a million dollars. When I told Joe about my childhood boast he smiled and said, "Sure you will, Frank." Then the conversation moved to some other topic.

Peter Waters helped revive my interest in politics, the interest my father had inspired years earlier. During the next municipal election I managed the corps of volunteers, whose work involved manning telephones and distributing pamphlets on Peter's behalf. When we won, I was so elated over the success and so confident in my rejection of alcohol that I volunteered to tend bar at the post-election victory party. As any recovering alcoholic can confirm, this was a risky move, but I never gave it a second thought—I was that confident in my resolve never to drink again. In the middle of the party, I looked up from pouring someone a double rye whisky to see a familiar face. The man, already well into his cups, was wearing a lopsided grin and waiting for me to recognize him. It was Bill Orr, the Oakville customer from my ill-fated career as a paint salesman two years earlier.

"You're not drinking," he noted, and I told him my story—the decision I made standing alone in the park two days before Christmas, my long trek up the stairs to meet Marg Meek, her simple greeting of "You're home," Joe's daily handful of dimes, and the support group that had kept me dry. When I finished, Bill stared into his empty glass before handing it to me. "Make the next one a double for the road," he said. "It'll be my last."

I assumed he meant his last drink of the night, but Bill meant it would be the last drink he ever had. And it was. If Peter and I could do it, Bill decided, he could do it as well. And he did.

PETER'S RE-ELECTION CAMPAIGN had been fun. I enjoyed the competition, the camaraderie, the teamwork, and the satisfaction of victory. The following spring, when a federal election was called, I volunteered to work on the campaign of a physician named Frank Philbrook, who was seeking nomination as the Liberal candidate in the riding of Halton. We set to work recruiting new party members, seeking endorsements from prominent local Liberals, and distributing literature to delegates. Frank and his opponent were evenly matched, and we needed an exceptional effort. If I ever had any doubts about my political instincts, working on Frank Philbrook's campaign erased them.

Halton was a massive riding, stretching more than forty kilometres north from Oakville and encompassing prosperous farms and quaint rural villages. The nomination meeting was held at the School for the Deaf in Milton, several kilometres up the road from our base in Oakville. As a promotional gimmick, I suggested that Frank greet delegates at the entrance to the hall and hand long-stemmed roses to every woman who arrived, thanking them for making the long trek to the meeting. Everyone agreed it was a fine idea, especially when we tied a ribbon bearing Frank Philbrook's name to every rose.

On nomination night, we arrived at the hall to discover our opponent's workers distributing shiny red apples to delegates. "It's a better idea," someone on our team muttered. "Only the women get roses, but everybody gets an apple. They're pulling both men *and* women to their side."

I wasn't so sure. True, the delegates were soon crunching into the opponent's apples, but once the fruit was consumed, what then? No one on the other side had given any thought to the disposal of the apple cores. The delegates looked around for garbage cans or some other place to discard the messy cores. When they saw none, many began wrapping them in tissues or just sat there holding a well-chewed apple that was already turning an unappetizing brown. Some slipped them under their chairs. To make things worse, it was an exceptionally warm night and the hall lacked air conditioning. The unpleasant smell of warm apples permeated the stagnant air through the speeches and voting procedures. Meanwhile, women delegates lifted their blooms to their noses, smiling at the pleasant floral scent. And they would be taking the roses home to enjoy for another few days.

I can't claim that winning the roses-versus-apples war earned our candidate the nomination, but he won a very close contest, the kind where annoyance over one opponent's faux pas might have veered a handful of votes in the other direction. I went home that night feeling that I might have tapped another talent, once again quietly amazed at how far I had come in such a short time.

Now that we had a candidate, our next job was to win the election. When Frank Philbrook asked me to fill the role of campaign manager, I eagerly accepted.

Securing the nomination had been an accomplishment, but grabbing a seat in Parliament for the Liberals in Halton would be a major challenge: The riding had elected Tories two out of three times since Confederation. We wouldn't just be unseating an incumbent, we would be practically overturning a century-old tradition. To complicate things, Frank was running against Terry O'Connor, a bright young lawyer. With Trudeaumania fading, Conservative Party leader Robert Stanfield looking very prime ministerial, and Halton voters seemingly uninterested in anyone but Tories, I knew unseating O'Connor would take more than a one-shot gimmick like ribbon-wrapped roses. It took several gimmicks, though I prefer to call them tactics.

Our first move was to take advantage of our campaign headquarters, in a former automotive dealership smack in the middle of downtown Oakville. The location was convenient and the building ideal, but its massive display windows presented us with a potential problem we needed to address.

Few events prove the adage about perception being reality better than election campaigns. No matter how many challenges your candidate may face, you must always maintain the aura of success. Whatever their political persuasion, voters prefer to support a winner, and their perception of a winner can and should be established long before they enter the polling booth.

That was the challenge posed by our high-profile headquarters. What would passersby think if they looked in to see only two or three volunteers pecking away at typewriters or talking on the telephone? What would be their perception of a dark, vacant office on days when all the campaign workers were away from headquarters canvassing door to door? I feared a gloomy and empty headquarters would suggest our campaign lacked energy and support. That's not how a winner appears.

Someone suggested we conceal the interior from the outside world by taping campaign posters to the plate glass windows. This would work fine when the place was empty, but on days when we wanted people to see a large contingent of workers inside, the positive message would be hidden. I had a better idea.

With no shortage of volunteers, I arranged a schedule that put several people in our headquarters, seated near the display windows, every afternoon and evening. Anyone passing by would see a small crowd of people chatting on telephones, addressing and licking envelopes, or discussing campaign strategy perhaps. If they were actually talking with their spouse, mailing their utility bills or trading cake recipes, it didn't matter. Our goal was to create the impression of a high-energy campaign, one that was full of life and bursting with enthusiasm. What's more, we wanted the other candidate's organization to absorb the message as much as the voters did, diverting the opposition from his long-term strategy to deal with our apparent success. From the day we officially opened the campaign headquarters, at least a dozen people could be seen working diligently in those oversized display windows on behalf of the Liberal candidate.

Mailings to voters are important in every election campaign, but the number of times you can stuff an envelope in a voter's mailbox is limited. A campaign that sends too many mailings wastes valuable financial resources and risks creating a backlash from voters over the volume of mail they're receiving from your campaign.

We couldn't afford to send multiple mailings anyway. But most of the envelopes the volunteers were addressing were never mailed. I needed to create a sense of urgency and vitality to the campaign, and I attracted young volunteers to campaign headquarters with pizza and Coca-Cola. Everybody was having fun. At the end of the night, I gathered up the scribbled-on envelopes and deposited them in trash bins all over town.

The media scuttlebutt in Halton began reporting that Frank Philbrook was running a vigorous campaign, and the Tory opponent could no longer take victory for granted. Nobody on the other side caught on to our ploy. Working with a lean crew of volunteers, the Tory headquarters was dark and empty by nine o'clock each night, a mausoleum compared with our location, where the lights burned, the radio played, and the crowd stayed until midnight. Our opponent grew demoralized by the sight, while voters were impressed by our positive spin. If Frank Philbrook could generate so much support, they speculated, there must be something to him, even if he was a Liberal.

We took advantage of every opportunity to draw attention to our candidate. One Sunday morning, I visited headquarters to attend a strategy session with the chairman of the finance committee, the guy assigned to raise money for the campaign. Looking in one direction from the headquarters window, I saw a crowd watching a soapbox derby race. Meanwhile, over in the other direction, I noticed our opponent was hosting a Meet the Candidate event at the home of one of his supporters. I had an idea.

I phoned the operator of the local ice-cream trucks, the ones that cruise the streets ringing bells and playing music to entice kids to the curb. If he sent his fleet to our headquarters right away, I promised, we would purchase each truck's entire stock of ice cream. Soon three vehicles were parked in front of our headquarters, handing out ice cream treats "Courtesy of your Liberal candidate, Frank Philbrook." We drew crowds not only from the soapbox derby but from our opponent's event, creating even more attention for our candidate.

The campaign proved a great success. Frank won handily, scoring a Liberal victory in a solid Tory riding. This was a significant achievement, marking yet another step in my journey from Lower Jarvis Street. It also led to a relationship that both rewarded and tested me in ways I could never have anticipated.

AT CAMPAIGN HEADQUARTERS that Sunday morning, I met with the finance committee chairman, Tom Culligan. I had encountered Tom in Toronto before working with him on Frank Philbrook's campaign. Tall, slim, fashionable, and smart—very, very smart—Tom grew up in a small New Brunswick village on Chaleur Bay, one of ten children born to a strong-willed mother and an alcoholic father who abandoned his family when Tom was just a boy. Our mutual Roman Catholic upbringing was one link between us, but an even stronger connection was the discovery that we shared the same birthdate: June 14, 1945.

Tom had seriously considered becoming a priest, and he earned degrees in theology and philosophy before abandoning religion in favour of a business career. When we met, he held an executive position with Cambridge Leaseholds, one of the country's largest and most successful operators of shopping malls. It's a mark of Tom's extraordinary talent and intelligence that, lacking any formal business education and not yet thirty years old, he was managing several of the largest shopping malls in Canada.

The election campaign was fun, but it had been like summer vacation in terms of our careers. Once our candidate was seated in Parliament, it was back to school for us, so to speak. Would we resume our jobs, me selling construction equipment, and Tom managing shopping malls? Neither one of us was enthusiastic about that option, and we soon began swapping business ideas. One day Tom said, "I think we should go into business together."

It seemed like a good plan. We had worked well together on the election campaign—maybe we could work just as well together as entrepreneurs. But what kind of business? Our only asset was a thousand-dollar Canada Savings Bond I had bought while selling construction equipment. Where would that get us? Not far.

We mentioned our predicament to Peter Waters, who had enticed me to Oakville in the first place, and he had an idea. "I know a guy who has a mail-order business selling coin sorters," Peter said. "If he gave you a sales territory, you wouldn't need much money to get started." Tom and I looked at each other and shrugged. Coin-sorting equipment hardly sounded like a road to riches, but we didn't have many alternatives, so why not try it?

Tom and I drove to Grimsby, midway between Toronto and Niagara Falls, to meet with Ron Gdanski. He demonstrated his sorting device for us. It was a brilliant design that used gravity to separate coins. You poured coins in the top and they flowed through channels to be collected at the bottom, divided into bins of pennies, nickels, dimes, and quarters. We liked the device's appearance and foolproof operation, but we liked the profit potential even more: The wholesale cost for each unit was $13, and it retailed for $39.95. Ron offered us all of Canada as a sales territory if we wanted it. We took it.

As former altar boys, Tom and I knew church bazaars, weekly bingo games, fundraising dinners, and of course, Sunday collection plates all generated baskets of coins for Catholic churches, and all required volunteer parishioners to separate and count—a tedious task. The expenditure to buy one or two coin sorters would quickly be approved. "Know your market" is a basic principle in any business, and we knew ours.

We created a one-page flyer promoting the product, printed a few hundred copies, and purchased envelopes and postage. Next, we visited the Oakville Public Library, borrowed a book listing the mailing addresses for Roman Catholic churches across Canada, and copied the information. Our first mailing was sent to about two dozen churches, and within a few days the cheques began to arrive. We cashed the cheques, bought the sorters from Ron, and shipped them to the customers. Our profits paid the rent, put food in our refrigerator, and covered the cost of mailing more flyers.

That's how things went for several weeks. Our little home-based business grew considerably when Ron offered us a sales territory in the United States. We were meeting our expenses with a little money left over, but neither the mail-order business nor the ecclesiastical market appealed to us for the long term. Something more promising would come along, we hoped—and it did, with a telephone call from Bill Seli, an executive at Trizec, another shopping mall operator. Bill had a question for Tom.

While with Cambridge, Tom had negotiated a lease with a husband-and-wife team who wanted to sell coffee beans from a kiosk in nearby Burlington Mall. The business seemed to be going well, Bill remembered. He had a similar space available in the centre of the food court at Scarborough Town Centre, a location that seemed ideal for a coffee bean retailer. Would Tom check with the couple to see if they were interested in expanding into the Toronto market?

Tom agreed. He visited the husband and wife, who responded with an emphatic "no." Tom wasn't surprised. Selling coffee beans was a dry goods operation with slim margins, considerable wastage, and questionable suppliers. Managing two kiosks in malls eighty kilometres apart would have been challenging for the couple to do successfully. But maybe, Tom suggested, he and I could operate one.

I have never met anyone who understood the retail business better than Tom Culligan. He knew Scarborough Town Centre was a prime mall, with more sales per square metre than most similar-sized operations in Canada. And he knew how the retail market worked. Neither one of us knew much about coffee, but Tom knew retail, I knew selling, and this was a rare opportunity. "I definitely think we should go into the coffee business," Tom said. Tom could be very persuasive. Besides, how difficult could it be? You stocked coffee, weighed it, bagged it, and sold it. I agreed, and within days we signed a lease.

We had Larry Funston, a well-regarded retail-space designer, create a kiosk that was barely forty-five square metres. We were on our way. It was August 1975.

Tom and I hadn't yet given any thought to naming our new business. We knew we should incorporate, however, so we called a lawyer named Harry Funk, whom Tom and I knew from the election campaign, to handle our legal needs. Harry reminded us that we needed a name for our fledgling operation before he could file the incorporation papers. "We'll get back to you," Tom said.

From Harry's office, we called another contact we had made during the election campaign. Jack Burkholder was a marketing whiz who coined the Esso slogan *Put a Tiger in Your Tank*. If he was good enough for Esso, Tom and I decided, he was good enough for us, and we phoned Jack at his home. "We need a name for our coffee business," Tom said. "Do you have any ideas?"

The best known coffee brand at the time was Maxwell House, and its slogan *Good to the Last Drop* was memorable. We wanted something just as distinctive. Tom and Jack tossed some ideas back and forth over the telephone while Jack's wife, Joan, watched television in their living room. An announcer's voice ended a TV commercial for Schaefer Beer by saying, "The one beer to have when you're having more than one." "Now there's a good slogan," Jack said when he heard it, and Joan, who had been listening to her husband's end of the conversation and knew he was searching for a name for our company, said, "So call it Second Cup."

[SIX]

Not the Biggest, But Certainly the First

We had a concept, a name, a paper corporation, space in a shopping mall, and not much else. In fact, we lacked several ingredients considered essential to running a business. Like product knowledge, for example.

We knew enough about coffee to recognize that Colombian beans were highly regarded, Hawaiian beans were expensive, Brazilian beans were low-priced, and dark beans had been roasted longer for a more intense flavour. Beyond that, nothing.

To fill the bins in our kiosk we searched the Yellow Pages, chose a coffee wholesaler listed there, and ordered our first shipment. Within a few days the beans arrived in paper sacks marked *Brazil, Costa Rica, Colombian,* and so on. We were in business.

We dumped the beans in the appropriate bins, set up our pricing chart, and began selling coffee at prices based on the wholesale cost—low for Brazil, higher for Colombian and Costa Rican.

We soon decided that we needed someone to help manage the kiosk and so, in a move that proved brilliant in hindsight, we hired a woman who knew more about coffee than we did. Much more. Arriving for her first day at work, she glanced at the bins, inspected the beans, and looked at us with some amusement. "They're all the same beans," she said. "Your supplier is putting the same cheap beans in different sacks and overcharging you!" It was our first major lesson in the coffee business and one we summed up as "Always hire smarter." Of course it's a rule every business should follow whatever their product or service.

Guided by her expertise, we dropped our supplier and contacted Claudio Basandri, who ran Club Coffee, a subsidiary of Nabisco. Claudio proved even more of a godsend than our part-time coffee expert. Thanks to his integrity and support, plus the high quality of his goods and the company's fair pricing, Claudio became our sole supplier. Together, Nabisco and Second Cup made a lot of money over the years, a tribute to the loyalty that good products and service can generate.

Tom's genius at retail strategy made an impact from the beginning. Once we had established a reasonable sales volume for our beans, Tom suggested we strengthen the brand by emblazoning coffee mugs with our logo, and broadening our product line with a wider selection of beans.

Customer service is the key to every retailing success, and we looked for ways to improve ours. One method was to maintain card files listing every customer's preference of coffee types and blends. If Mary Smith preferred a blend of two-thirds French Roast and one-third Costa Rican, this information was filed under her name and became Mary Smith's blend. In the age of personal computers, this system would be easy to implement, but the manual card method led to numerous problems. Eventually, we dropped the system, but retained the concept of personalized service wherever possible. It was a learn-as-you-go experience, and we learned a great deal—enough to open a second kiosk in Toronto and a third in Ottawa.

We may have been learning about the coffee business, but we had yet to learn how to calculate our profit, or in this case our losses. Without a bookkeeper, which we felt we couldn't afford, we were unable to balance costs against sales, and while both were growing at a steady rate, the former were outstripping the latter. In fact, the only thing keeping us solvent was selling the coin sorters, a source of cash that dried up when a strike by Canada Post cut off our distribution in both Canada and the United States for thirteen weeks. Halfway through the postal strike, with no income from our mail-order operation, the true state of our coffee business became clear, and it wasn't pretty. We needed to inject life into Second Cup or it would slide to the same dead end as our coin-sorter business.

Tom and I were discussing the problem one day as we walked through the mall's food court. Spotting the Baskin-Robbins outlet, Tom decided he wanted an ice-cream cone. Unable to make up his mind, he sampled first one flavour and then another, before choosing a third. Waiting for our cones, Tom turned to me and said, "You know, I just sampled ice cream. Why can't we have people sample our coffee? Once they taste how good it is, they would buy some beans to take home."

"Would that work?" I asked.

"Grocery stores sample products all the time," Tom pointed out. "If it works for jams and crackers and ice cream, why won't it work for coffee? People could taste our decaf, our expensive Colombian, the dark French Roast, and buy the one they like best. We would also be able to demonstrate a connection between price and quality. When you do that, people start paying a little more for a difference they can identify, and that widens the sales margins."

As we ate our ice cream, we continued building on the germ of this idea. People had been selling quality coffee beans for some time, but no one had chosen to sell coffee that had been brewed from the beans they were selling. We didn't know it at the time, but that conversation in front of the ice-cream counter was building the foundation for an industry that would soon sweep across North America.

Like all ideas after they have proven successful, brewing and selling coffee from specialized outlets sounds obvious today, when they are ubiquitous, but in the mid-1970s, high-quality coffee retailers were non-existent. Most people either settled for instant coffee at home or drank it in a restaurant along with their lunch and dinner. In fact, through the 1960s and 1970s, the bestselling coffee in North America was a freeze-dried concoction that turned from a powder into a dark liquid with the addition of hot water. Any resemblance to first-rate real coffee was coincidental.

Prepared coffee was made by food outlets from nondescript beans of only passable quality, with more emphasis on keeping costs down than setting high standards. If you wanted a great cup of coffee, you brewed it at home after going through the exercise of choosing the beans, grinding them, and brewing them in a coffeemaker. There was no middle ground.

What's more, in the 1970s, the market for coffee was declining. Fewer people were drinking it because most of the prepared stuff was awful, and brewing your own was a tedious process. Consumers expected the coffee they drank outside their homes to be little more than hot, dark, and cheap. With expectations so limited, convenience became more of a factor, which explains why those years marked a major growth in instant-coffee sales. People had forgotten what good coffee was all about, how satisfying it could be. Coffee had become an ancillary product, something you ordered along with your sandwich or burger or fried chicken. More often than not, it was brewed from the cheapest beans available and poured from a pot that had been sitting on a hot burner for hours. Because expectations were low, complaints about quality were few, and aspects such as flavour and aroma were unimportant.

Tim Hortons was still a small chain targeting working-class patrons, growing out of its roots in the industrialized area of Hamilton, Ontario, and located for the most part in former gasoline stations converted into doughnut shops. Hortons sold a single blend of coffee whose primary function was to accompany the doughnuts that were the brand's chief appeal.

And what of that global behemoth Starbucks, the Wal-Mart of coffee? In the mid-1970s, Starbucks was a local operation run by two teachers and a writer, selling beans and coffee-making machines. If you wanted first-rate coffee, you bought beans and a machine from Starbucks and carted them home yourself. Not until 1985, when a new partner named Howard Schultz launched a series of coffee bars dubbed "Il Gionale" did Starbucks offer fresh-brewed coffee, and it took two more years before the

Starbucks name appeared on a cup of java. By that time, Second Cup was well into its second decade. So all of this came long after Tom and I set out to do nothing less than change the market. Our coffee would always be fresh, the beans would always be grade-A quality, and the final product would always be made according to standards that no restaurant brew could hope to match. We were venturing into uncharted territory.

We agreed that our samples would not be free; customers would pay for each cup they consumed, and we would offer coffee in the customer's choice of mild, medium, or strong strengths. Second Cup would carry a premium price to reflect its quality and establish a perceived value level based on "You get what you pay for." Everyone else was charging twenty-five cents for a cup of coffee. We would charge thirty-five cents for the same cup size, and we would justify the higher price with exceptional quality and consistency. This all sounds obvious today, but at the time these marketing methods were revolutionary.

Talking about concepts was easy. Dealing with reality was difficult. To brew coffee, we faced another hurdle: None of our kiosks had running water, a problem we solved by purchasing five-gallon containers at Canadian Tire and schlepping water from the sink in the stock room to our kiosk—which we did for over a year.

But we had a winner. From almost the first day, lineups began to form at Second Cup kiosks. People were learning the difference between coffee freshly brewed from superior beans and sludge that sat on a burner all day. We fulfilled our promise of quality by tossing out any coffee that wasn't sold within thirty minutes of being brewed, a then unheard-of policy.

Second Cup was a revelation to people who first tried it. No longer an afterthought, our coffee became a beverage to be savoured. In many ways, we re-educated consumers to the original appeal of coffee, away from the artificial taste of instant coffee and the burnt flavour of the percolated version. On a wider scale, we launched a branded industry, something rarely achieved by any new business venture, and helped speed the decline of instant-coffee sales.

Naturally, Tom and I were elated over our success, but it wasn't long before I was brought down to earth. "So tell me, Frank," I heard a man say as I poured coffee for a customer. "How are you going to make your million dollars out of this?" The voice belonged to Joe Green, the construction equipment salesman to whom I had revealed my dream of becoming a millionaire before I was thirty-five years old.

Joe hadn't meant his comment to be malicious, but I was embarrassed nevertheless. My confidence and self-esteem were higher than when I had been panhandling on Jarvis Street, but both remained fragile. After years of being destined for defeat, it would take many more years for all my emotional scars to heal. As I watched Joe walk away with his coffee, I realized that part of me agreed with him. How many cups of thirty-five-cent coffee does it take to pocket a million dollars? The math was too daunting, the dream too outrageous.

I needed to build my confidence, a quality Tom never lacked. I may have had doubts about becoming a coffee millionaire, but Tom had none at all, and at his insistence we began sketching a vision of our future. Someday, we determined, hundreds of Second Cup outlets located coast to coast in Canada would be spinning off profits. That was our target, and working toward it kept us going through the darker periods.

As time passed, we found ways to finesse the original concept, refining it to increase customer appeal. Instead of labelling our coffee simply mild, medium, and strong, we added the sources and blends of the beans, along with descriptions of their character. They became, for example, Mild Costa Rican, Medium Colombian, and Strong French Roast. By changing the blends from time to time, we invited customers to sample different flavours and identify their personal favourites.

This sophistication in coffee quality and flavour created new social and economic realities for our business. When customers began to enjoy coffee for its own sake, they sought to share the experience with others, adapting some of the counterculture coffee-house atmosphere of the 1960s to the suburban commercial environment. When we saw how people wanted to share their Second Cup coffee with friends, we added chairs and tables to our outlets, encouraging them to linger and relax. This move made our original kiosks impractical, so we relocated into store-sized units that had their own water supply and cleaning facilities, absorbing the extra cost with higher-volume sales and food items to be consumed with the coffee—biscotti, muffins, and tarts (but no doughnuts).

Again, all of this sounds obvious, now that half a dozen national chains have built their success using the same strategy, but thirty-plus years ago the ideas were radical. In my opinion, and the opinion of others in the industry, all the purveyors of premium coffee, and the multibillion-dollar-a-year industry they generated, can trace their origins to that conversation Tom and I had while eating ice-cream cones in front of Baskin-Robbins.

[SEVEN]

Lessons in Politics, Business, and Friendship

Politics teaches you many things, including how to be gracious in both victory and defeat. The lessons, by the way, don't have to be direct to be learned. They can also be acquired by working with and watching others, as I discovered a couple of years later.

In the midst of building Second Cup, Tom and I decided to re-enter the political arena when a friend invited us to work on behalf of a candidate for the 1976 Progressive Conservative leadership campaign. Politics is indeed in the blood of some people; although my most recent association had been with the federal Liberal party, I couldn't resist the challenge.

The candidate was Paul Hellyer, a former Liberal who had lost to Pierre Trudeau in 1968. Leaving the Liberals, Hellyer first attempted to launch a new political party called Action Canada, before settling down as a columnist for the *Toronto Sun*. Politics apparently ran even more thickly in Hellyer's veins than in my own because, when Robert Stanfield agreed to step down as PC leader, Hellyer threw a hat in the ring—not his own hat, however.

The strategy went like this: Tory MP Sean O'Sullivan (who would play a role in my entry into public service work many years later) had joined forces with Jake Epp, another MP, to set up an organization ostensibly backing Epp as a leadership candidate. Once the structure was in place, Epp would step aside in favour of Hellyer. In this way, Hellyer could continue working as a political columnist for the *Sun* until his candidacy was officially announced.

I found Hellyer an interesting guy, and when I was offered the position as his aide, travelling across the country with him to meet delegates and promote his candidacy, I quickly accepted.

At Hellyer's first meeting with his organization, he set the budget for his leadership campaign at $600,000. "That's the absolute maximum," he told us. "If one more dollar will ensure my election, don't spend it. We'll have to make do with six hundred thousand."

In 1976, $600,000 was a substantial amount of money for a political leadership campaign, and I was impressed by Hellyer's insistence that it would have to do. Of course, it didn't do. And the budget didn't stop there either. By the end of the campaign, we had spent twice that amount. That was my first lesson: Political campaigns are impossible to control; events take over, and all you can do is hold on for the ride.

On the eve of the convention vote, we were confident of success. Media polls indicated that Claude Wagner, himself a former Liberal and a provincial cabinet minister, was leading, with newcomer Brian Mulroney running second. Both were Quebec-based candidates, and many people expected them to split the support from that province. Joe Clark and Flora MacDonald represented the Red Tories, those Conservatives whose political position was closer to the Liberals, and were given little chance of succeeding. Clark appeared too wishy-washy against powerhouses like Wagner and Mulroney, and no one was prepared to elect a woman as party leader.

As the convention proceeded that first day in Ottawa's Exhibition Place, everyone on Hellyer's team believed he would emerge as the victor. Our man had impressed many delegates, and we had worked hard on his behalf. In a few days, Paul Hellyer could very well stand in the House of Commons as Leader of Her Majesty's Loyal Opposition, with an excellent prospect of becoming prime minister as Trudeaumania continued to wane.

Then came my second lesson.

In an attempt to pull the right wing of the party into his fold, Hellyer, a centrist, criticized Red Tories during his speech. As a strategy concocted in a backroom somewhere it may have made sense, but from the podium it proved a disaster. He was booed loudly and derisively by the party's left wing, and any chance we had for victory vanished in the smoky air above the delegate floor. To almost everyone's surprise, Joe Clark won the leadership. Claude Wagner went back to Quebec, Flora MacDonald returned to Kingston, and Brian Mulroney began plotting Clark's overthrow, which he accomplished six years later. And every Hellyer supporter vanished with the wind. Of the dozens of people who had been clapping Hellyer's back a few days earlier, only I remained behind to drive him home. I learned, as every politician and political strategist must, that months of effort and millions of dollars cannot overcome the impact of a few poorly chosen words at an inopportune time.

Fortunately, I also learned a third lesson.

Hellyer returned home to find a message from Doug Creighton, his publisher at the *Sun*. After giving his condolences, Creighton told Hellyer that his job as a newspaper columnist was still waiting for him if he wanted it. The day after missing a chance at arguably the second most important political post in Canada, Paul was back in the press gallery with the rest of the "ink-stained wretches" watching, listening, and reporting as Joe Clark accepted congratulations on his victory. It was a courageous, classy thing to do.

RETURNING TO FULL-TIME MANAGEMENT of Second Cup, we encountered a near disastrous situation. We were virtually bankrupt. Without our hands on the tiller, the company had drifted. Bills were unpaid, sales were down, and suppliers were threatening legal action. We contacted our creditors to negotiate settlements and offer postdated cheques for payment.

All but one of our suppliers agreed to this arrangement. The hold-out, who we discovered wanted an introduction into the retail business, insisted on attaching our three Second Cup outlets as security. He expected us to fail, and if we did, he would gain a quick, cheap, and easy entry into the retail coffee business. With no alternative, we agreed to the supplier's demand, paid off the debt as quickly as we could, and never dealt with the firm again. Then we set to work building Second Cup into a national chain, rewarding both ourselves and the suppliers who had expressed trust in us.

While Tom Culligan possessed retail brilliance, the growth and success of Second Cup was very much a team affair, with both of us sharing equally in management decisions. Our success, as limited as it was in the early years, enabled each of us to clearly identify our strengths and management philosophies. My approach was rather methodical, reflecting my Hope, Vision, Action philosophy. I tended to be reflective, weighing pros and cons to determine the best approach, before persuading others to come onside. Many innovations originated with me, though often they were implemented only after lengthy efforts to convince Tom that the idea was worth trying.

Tom acted more directly, shifting his direction almost instantaneously if his original idea wasn't working. He was more narrowly focused on the business than I was, and as contradictory as it sounds, he was also more conservative and yet more impulsive in his management style. Our abilities complemented each other, but they also generated friction from time to time. If a new idea came up, I would say, "Let's kick that around," while Tom would say either "Let's *do* it!" or "Forget it!" If a problem with an employee arose, I said "Let's talk to him" where Tom's reaction was "Fire the guy!"

Our expansion did not go unnoticed. Timothy's Coffees of the World soon duplicated our strategy, opening mall locations offering a similar product line to ours. But Timothy's invited customers to pour their own coffee; at Second Cup, we insisted on pouring it for them. A small point, perhaps, but this was a distinction we retained. We also paid attention to details in the decor and ambience, painting our locations with attractive colours that reflected the warm and inviting nature of our coffee. All in all, I think we did things better than our competition, and our growth, especially in the first few years, confirms it.

SUCCESSFUL WE MIGHT HAVE BEEN, but wealthy we were not. The entire operation, after all, had been financed with my thousand-dollar Canada Savings Bond, parlaying profit from the coin-sorter sales first into the coffee kiosks and later into the larger locations. And so, we remained undercapitalized. On some mornings, the only breakfast Tom and I could afford was a cup of coffee from one of our own outlets.

By the late 1970s, we needed to expand beyond the seven stores we were operating if we were to fulfill our vision for the company. One of our most successful stores had been in Toronto's Eaton Centre, and when Eaton Centre management offered a second site in a newly opened wing of the mall, we jumped at the opportunity. Our existing capital was too slim to cover the cost of building and equipping this new site, so we visited our bank, the one with a green sign, for a loan. The branch manager listened to our proposition, studied our financial records for a few moments, and then shook his head. "We think," he said, with the expression bankers display when turning down a loan, "that your seven stores have saturated the market for coffee in Canada. We just don't believe there is room for more outlets like yours. Sorry."

We were stunned. Did he honestly believe that the country could support only seven premium coffee outlets? Apparently he did. Tom and I didn't even try to convince him that he was wrong. Instead, we walked out of his office and down the street to the next bank, which had a blue-and-gold sign. After we introduced ourselves, showed the manager our financial records, outlined our business plan, and made our pitch, the bank manager said, "Sounds good to me." A short time later, the papers were signed, and we moved all of our business to that bank. As it had with our friend Claudio Basandri, the trustworthy coffee supplier, this decision made a lot of money for both sides over the years.

While all of this was happening, the shopping mall industry was entering a period of enormous expansion across Canada, and this proved a major boost to our growth. New malls needed new tenants, and Second Cup was proving attractive to mall operators everywhere. We were a class act, we paid our bills, and we encouraged shoppers to linger at the mall, all of which made us a prime tenant. The opportunity to expand could not be ignored, but it wouldn't last forever: We needed to act before one of the copycat operations elbowed us out.

Financing the expansion ourselves was out of the question. The capitalization to cover our costs would have been huge, requiring us to partner with a large source of cash or take the company public, and neither option was attractive. Management costs for a centralized operation with company-owned outlets would be crippling. Although Second Cup locations were averaging about $250,000 in annual sales— a substantial amount in 1978–80 dollars—running a national network would have drained our cash flow in head-office expenses alone. There had to be an alternative.

We agreed that hiring district managers or taking the time to fly here and there to supervise a cross-country network was out of the question. Yet, if we failed to take advantage of the expansion opportunities, someone else would do it, using our success as a blueprint. The only answer was franchising. Selling franchises would enable us to keep our head office staff small, eliminate the need for a massive infusion of capital, and still maintain standards of quality and service that everyone could adhere to. We faced a serious problem, however; we knew even less about franchising than we had known about the coffee business.

Once again, we were fortunate to connect with an outstanding source of expertise. While researching the franchise industry, Tom and I were introduced to Bob Harris, a lawyer who owned a few franchise operations himself. He had also drafted agreements for franchisors, and the experience he gained from working both sides of the table was priceless. Over hours of consulting, Bob taught us about franchising, including how to phrase the contracts so that they were accurate, clear, and fair to both franchisor and franchisee.

Tom and I sharpened the division between our respective responsibilities: He would focus on running the retail side of the business, and I would concentrate on the legal and franchising sides of the business. Once the paperwork between Second Cup and the franchisee was completed, I would pass the franchisee on to Tom, who proved to be a first-rate trainer. Tom's training ensured that every new franchise operator was capable of duplicating the standards Tom and I had set for the company. We became a formidable team, and the clear separation of responsibilities made it easier for us to work together.

Franchisees can be difficult to deal with, but their attitude is understandable when you consider the facts. It takes both an entrepreneurial attitude and a good deal of faith, after all, to write a cheque for $50,000, $100,000, $500,000, or more and hand it to a near stranger before you've made your first sale. You have to believe in yourself, and you have to be driven to succeed. That's the kind of strong-willed and ambitious people we were looking for as franchisees. Of course, these same qualities tend to produce a streak of rebellion in the same individuals, one that eventually convinces them that they know more than those fools back at head office, and that head office is making more money off the franchisee's labour than it deserves.

This can lead to a love–hate relationship as passionate as any marriage. Once the first warm feelings between franchisor and franchisee have faded, it's not long before one side suspects the other of being unfaithful. I learned to expect emotional outbursts, and I insisted that every new franchisee expect them as well. Whenever I was closing a franchise deal, I showed the franchisee a graph. "Dependency" was charted on the vertical y-axis, "Time" on the horizontal x-axis. The graph showed a line that began at the top of the dependency axis, then swooped down so low it almost touched the time axis running along the bottom of the page before swooping back up to complete the U shape. "This is what's going to happen in the first year we're together," I would say, indicating the low point of the curve. "After ten or twelve months, you'll start believing you know more about this business than we do, and that we don't deserve our fees and royalties. You'll want to shed your dependency on us, and it may take a while for you to realize it's not a wise move." I would then point to where the line began ascending. "If you can hang on until here, when you have the complete picture, things will start getting better, and you will achieve true interdependence."

Few believed me but, almost without fail, I would receive a phone call after several months, a call that often began with the new franchisee calling me nasty names. After giving the franchisee time to vent his or her anger, I would say: "Do you know where you are on the dependency graph I showed you? You're at the bottom, exactly where and when I predicted you would be." From there, we would start rebuilding our relationship—toward the upward-climbing side of the U.

Our franchise operations unfolded smoothly, with the exception of the odd and unexpected speed bump. One involved a junior executive with IBM who saw a brighter future as a Second Cup franchisee than a lifetime with Big Blue, his original idea. We were about to sew up a deal when IBM transferred him to Calgary, and he decided to stay with the computer firm.

I wished him well and considered the matter closed, but six months later, he phoned from Alberta to announce that he had left IBM and wanted to open a Second Cup franchise in Calgary. We picked up our negotiations where we had left off, discussing franchise fees, royalties, suppliers, the usual details, but within a few minutes, he began referring to our conditions as "typical of you bastards from the east!" What the heck was that all about?

The guy had launched his business career in Toronto, and six months after hitting Calgary he was referring to easterners as bastards?

Things eventually settled down, we signed the contracts, and soon the franchisee was working under the franchise arrangements we had agreed on.

One of our rules required franchisees to purchase coffee from our approved supplier exclusively. This had everything to do with quality control and customer satisfaction and nothing to do with squeezing the franchisee by forcing him or her to overpay for coffee, no matter what the franchisee might think. Top-quality coffee is not as common as many of our franchisees believed. Somebody is always in the market with a supply of low-quality beans, ready to dump them at a price significantly below that of the top-drawer product we specified. We insisted on coffee that measured up to Second Cup standards for freshness, and there could be no exceptions.

Our man in Calgary couldn't resist saving a few bucks from every discounter who showed up with a load of coffee, most of which was awful. When we learned about this, Tom responded in his usual manner. He hopped a flight to Calgary, confirmed the coffee was substandard, loaded it in a wagon, and tossed every gram into the nearest trash bin. The franchisee sued us, but the case was thrown out of court. We had made our point, and problems with substandard coffee beans, at that franchise at least, were laid to rest.

Much of our energy was spent trying to prevent franchisees from making silly, even self-destructive, decisions. The Second Cup franchise in a large Winnipeg mall is an excellent illustration of this. The operator had good sales volumes at his location, we had a good franchisee, and the mall had a good tenant. It all fell to pieces when the mall expanded and suggested relocating the Second Cup franchise to its new wing once the location lease expired, a few months later. I thought it was a great opportunity: The new wing was attractive and would draw more traffic. With rent and other costs unchanged, relocating would be beneficial for all of us. At least, that's the way Tom and I saw it. The franchisee saw things differently. He refused to move, under any conditions.

"I'm staying," he told me.

"I think you should take the offer," I responded. "In fact, I insist on it."

"This is where I started, and this is where I'm staying," the franchisee said adamantly.

"It's crazy," the mall operator said when he called me. "He'll make more sales in the new location, and it's not going to cost him a penny. If he doesn't move, we won't renew his lease, because we have plans for his spot."

I tried to talk sense into the franchisee. "If you let your lease expire, they'll evict you," I said. "You'll not only lose your location, you'll lose your franchise—it's in the agreement." There was no question about our intention to force the agreement, because we owned the master lease, and we refused to side with him over the dispute.

"I don't want to move," he told me when I called one last time to plead with him to accept the mall's offer.

"A newer environment, more shopper traffic, no increase in cost—what's not to like?" I argued.

"I won't move," the franchisee said stubbornly.

"They'll evict you," I pointed out.

"Then I'll sue the bastards."

One minute after midnight on the day the lease expired, a forklift drove through the mall, picked up the Second Cup kiosk and dumped it unceremoniously in the parking lot. The franchisee's lawsuit came to nothing. If the franchisee believed the move would cost him sales, even though all indications were that his sales and profits would grow, he could have sold the franchise and pocketed a profit. But he didn't, and his attitude cost him at least $400,000.

By the early 1980s, Second Cup boasted more than seventy outlets, both company-owned and franchised, across Canada. My thousand-dollar Canada Savings Bond had spawned a mail-order coin-sorter business that had rolled into a coffee kiosk that had morphed into a leading-edge marketing phenomenon that had expanded into a national corporation worth several million dollars.

Tom and I lived well, if not extravagantly.

He bought a lovely old Oakville mansion, in which he took great pride. I began exploring some long-held ambitions, including my dream of obtaining a pilot's licence. Owning and flying my own airplane had not been an obsessive goal, but now that it was within my reach, I decided to go ahead. With both the time and the means, I obtained my licence, bought an airplane, and took up flying the way other people take up golf. The sense of freedom I experienced flying was as liberating as anything I had done over the past few years. I could cruise literally a mile above the streets that had claimed many of my friends and had almost claimed me.

Success in business also led to a reconciliation of sorts with my family. I sought out my brothers and sister, attempting to make up in some way for the pain I had caused them. My brother Sean and I became reacquainted, and I discovered he possessed exceptional management skills. I introduced him to Tom, who was suitably impressed—and Tom was not an easy guy to impress—and soon Sean came aboard Second Cup, where he proved brilliant at identifying good locations and negotiating leases.

Things were not nearly as sanguine with my parents. My father, crushed by the failure of the company he had launched, sold the family home and he and Mother moved to our cottage in Lakefield, Quebec. His embarrassment over his business failure was so intense that he became something of a recluse, cutting off many friends and business associates he had gained over the years. For a man who had revelled in the joy of social contact, this must have been a terrible experience.

I sent him money from time to time and visited when I could. We spent many afternoons sitting on the cottage veranda having friendly, relaxed discussions about politics and business, and those times we spent together softened the pain, I'm sure, that we both carried from my adolescent days.

Dad knew of my success, of course, but he never directly acknowledged it. Later, I learned that he told others, expressing his pride not only in my business achievements but in my personal accomplishments as well.

Confirmation of his faith in me and his pride in my success came almost too late for both of us. Soon after we reconciled, in our awkward manner, Dad began suffering from emphysema. The disease weakened his heart, and within a short time he suffered a massive heart attack and died in the hospital.

Everyone is changed by the death of a parent, sometimes in an unforeseen way. I recalled my mixed emotions at being able to give my father money when he needed it. I took some pleasure in the fact that I had the resources to help him, even while I was saddened by his plight. The first role model that life had offered me had been desperate enough to need my assistance.

Many mourners attended his funeral. The chapel was overflowing with people who had known and loved my father during his successful years but whom he had been too humiliated by his company's bankruptcy to continue seeing. Their attendance, and the affection and thanks they expressed to the family, proved that he had been wrong to believe they would think less of him for his business difficulties.

I cried openly at his funeral, the first time in many years that I had shed tears. I cried not for my loss but for Dad's. I cried especially because he had underestimated his own standing among the people whose respect he valued, and because of his mistaken belief that one failure negated all the successes he had achieved in his life.

After I returned to Oakville, a familiar emotion began to settle in me. It was fear. With Dad's death came a fear that my life might end as his had, that the success I achieved might dissolve into failure, and that I too might need someone's charity. I hated that thought. I feared that possibility.

Dad's death sparked a remarkable change in my mother. She adored her husband and, choosing to remain in his shadow, had concealed throughout her married life her talents and abilities, revealing them only after our father's death. Alone for the first time in forty years, she seemed to emerge from a cocoon and spread her wings. She became a champion of the historical society, applying her energy and organizational abilities to the preservation and appreciation of community landmarks. This attracted the attention of local politicians and she was persuaded to seek election as a town councillor. She won the seat and, soon, her French-Canadian heritage overrode the Anglo persona she had assumed throughout her marriage. In council debates, and during the 1980 referendum on Quebec independence, she was vocal and persuasive. Her political stance even attracted the attention of the local Liberal MP Claude Ryan, who became a good friend.

I was so pleased for her, so touched by this new woman I saw, that I financed an extension to her cottage, giving her room to enjoy life in greater comfort. It was also, I suppose, a means of expressing my regret at all the sorrow and pain I had caused her, and an attempt to gain her approval. She accepted my generosity somewhat passively, neither rejecting it nor showing much enthusiasm for it. Then, in one of those ironies of life that teach us lessons we should already know, at the peak of her achievements she was diagnosed with pancreatic cancer.

We took her to a Montreal hospital, but everyone knew it was hopeless. All we could do was manage her pain while the cancer took its course. She was moved to my sister's home in Montreal, where Maureen provided round-the-clock loving care. I was present as often as possible, along with Maureen and my brothers. We did our best to make her comfortable, which was all we could do.

With Mother's death imminent, I felt compelled to make amends, to let her know that her son regretted all the pain and heartache he had caused her and Dad. One cool, grey Sunday night, I sat next to her bed and in a rambling manner told her I was sorry. I was sorry about not being a good student in school, sorry about the cars I had wrecked and the money I had stolen from her purse, sorry about not making her proud of me, and sorry about failing her and Dad and myself in so many ways.

When I finished, I let all my words settle around us.

After several minutes of silence, Mother spoke, her eyes closed. I couldn't hear her words at first. Or perhaps I could, and they didn't register. I leaned forward and asked her to repeat them.

"I'll never forgive you," she said.

[EIGHT]

A Matter of Trust and a Tale of Picassos

The death of parents changes our perception of the world and our place in it. Suddenly, our own mortality is no longer just a rumour. I returned from my mother's funeral looking at my life in a different way.

Tom and I were ten years into our business relationship. The company was doing well, spectacularly well in fact, but other things weren't nearly as good. I had made my million dollars, on paper at least, and that was gratifying. The relationship between Tom and me was less so.

Like everyone else at Second Cup, I had to deal with Tom's domineering personality, which I accepted as a by-product of his intellect and intensity. At first, I had little difficulty handling this trait, and as Second Cup grew, I came to value his dedication to reaching all the goals we set for ourselves and our business. We participated equally in managing the firm, though Tom's vision of the company culture was more rigid than mine. This rigidity grew out of his talent for retailing, for understanding not just what customers want but how they want it provided, at what price, and in what environment. Tom's retail focus drove most of his outlook and strategy, while I found myself more concerned with broader issues, including employee and franchisee relations.

In the beginning, the balance worked; we each brought important skills to the operation. Tom's leadership skills were generally superb because he was able to translate his vision into actions that the rest of us would undertake. He demanded attention from everyone around him, a quality that all leaders share, though some carry it off better than others. I acknowledged Tom's talent in these areas when we were business partners and I acknowledge it now. The more the company expanded, however, the more certain aspects of Tom's personality began to grate on me.

I began to notice how Tom, in pursuit of victory at any cost, could take a position completely opposite to one he had held just a few days or even a few hours earlier. He was capable of making a full 180-degree turn and claiming that he had been looking in that direction all along, no matter how much you reminded him of his previous position. Nor would he brook any disagreement with his claim. He was right and you were wrong, end of story.

Tom's methods of handling people could be disturbing. It became a joke at Second Cup that the worst career news you could receive was that Tom had given you a promotion, because it meant you were about to be fired. Did Tom feel so guilty about handing out pink slips that he tried to soften the impact by first flattering the employee with a promotion? Perhaps. I never fully understood his motivation.

Within the company, I was considered more approachable than Tom, a role that I felt comfortable playing. The good cop–bad cop approach is not unusual in partnerships, and ours worked for a time. Eventually, however, I began to believe that Tom's total fixation on the company's success and his heavy-handed management tactics were having a negative impact on staff performance and the future of Second Cup. Some companies need a hatchetman, but Tom's methods were making me increasingly uncomfortable. We rarely raised our voices to each other, though disagreements arose, as you might expect. Many of these resulted from my various activities outside the company, something that Tom seemed to grow to resent. Finally, things came to an impasse.

I had become an active supporter of self-help programs similar to the one that had aided me in getting off the street many years earlier. I knew that men and women who suffered from alcoholism as I had needed assistance to overcome their addiction and restore their self-confidence. I owed it to them to help, as both an example and a benefactor.

Combining my personal experience with my sales talents, I became an in-demand speaker at presentations dealing with alcohol addiction, and when an invitation arrived for me to address a gathering of over twenty thousand people at a conference in Louisiana, I felt honoured. Twenty thousand people who, like me, had once had nothing more than a glimmer of hope would hear my tale. I could stand in front of them and share the story of my journey with them, and I considered it a great honour to do so.

Tom grew resentful of the publicity my appearance at the conference was creating. After questioning the wisdom of my being absent from the business for several days, he placed so many demands on my schedule that it became impossible for me to make the journey to Louisiana and still fulfill my duties for the company. I was forced to cancel the speech.

Tom's motivation was clear. We were, on paper and in practical terms, equal partners, yet my public profile had grown substantially more than his. One of Tom's weaknesses was that he considered public recognition a zero-sum game, similar to the way he approached business generally. Whatever degree of success I achieved within Second Cup was a measure of personal failure to him. And however much fame I earned was somehow subtracted from his own self-worth. I thought this foolish, and I could barely conceal my anger at his unfairness.

These difficulties not only soured things between the two of us, they also affected the company. Tom was now aware that most staff members preferred to deal with me rather than him, and this made his relationship with the staff rockier than ever.

I became convinced that Second Cup had a better chance of succeeding with only one of us at the helm. I intended this to be me, and decided I would be the one to initiate it. I would buy Tom out.

I wish I could say that my concern for the company we had built up over the years and the welfare of the people who worked for us were my sole motivation for reaching this conclusion. And they were, to a degree. You cannot create an entity as successful, innovative, and widely admired as Second Cup was without feeling an immense amount of ownership and identity with it.

This identity, as things turned out, became a serious challenge for me to overcome.

In truth, however, Tom's and my working relationship was by now a mess, and it was poisoning the air between us. We were annoying each other too frequently, getting on each other's nerves over matters that we had once been able to resolve with no difficulty. To put it bluntly, Tom was pissing me off, and I wanted to manage the company on my own. I convinced myself this was no mere ego trip. Nor was it a decision driven by greed. I believed I was better at motivating the staff than Tom, and I was more of a risk-taker, more entrepreneurial in my approach to business. Tom, I concluded, was too conservative in his decision making, so focused on the retail side of the business that he had difficulty seeing the big picture. If Second Cup was to fulfill its potential, it needed a leader who was more open to new ideas than he was. I believed it was me.

By the spring of 1985, the market value of Second Cup was assessed at several million dollars, and Tom and I each owned 50 percent of those assets. I decided to offer Tom half the assessed value for his share of the company. If he accepted, it would leave me in sole control. And I was certain he would accept.

I approached the law firm of Fraser Milner, where Purdy Crawford headed a team to prepare the buyout offer. The lawyers located a source for the cash I would have to pay Tom for his share of the company. Believing in my heart that Tom was ready to move on to some other challenge, and demonstrating perhaps an inordinate amount of good faith and personal interest in his well-being, I sweetened the offer by reducing the price of my half of the company, should Tom choose to submit a buyout offer to counter my own, and offered access to my source of capital if he chose that option.

Everything was in place. All I had to do was present Tom with the offer, obtain his approval, write him the cheque, and assume total control. One day that summer, with my offer in hand, I sat down with Tom in his office and made my pitch.

"We've been together ten years," I began. "We've accomplished more than either of us could have predicted or even dreamed when we met, but I think we've come to a parting of ways." I told him I had plans for Second Cup, plans that I wanted to implement on my own, without his participation.

"Tom," I said, "I have a firm offer here to buy your share of the company."

There was no reaction.

I handed the proposal across the desk to him. "The details are in here. Let me know what you think when you've had a chance to study it."

Looking back, I don't believe he was entirely shocked at the news. Tom was always cool, after all. The only reaction I recall was a simple nod of his head. Then he studied the offer.

The original partnership agreement did not include a shotgun clause, intended to avoid an impasse when one of two equal partners wants out of a business arrangement. This should have been in place from the beginning, but it had never occurred to us to arrange the dissolution of our company while we were still busy building it.

With a shotgun clause, the partner being asked to sell his or her portion of the company must choose one of two alternatives: accept the money and walk away, or turn the offer around and purchase the other partner's share for the same amount of money. It's a clever way of ensuring that a fair price is available to both; if one partner underprices the offer, the other gets a bargain by invoking the clause.

I had permitted my feelings to override my business sense when drafting my offer to Tom. I felt guilty about being the one to initiate the move, which was why I reduced the price of my half of the company by $50,000 if Tom chose to purchase my half instead of selling me his portion. With an agreement that he could draw capital from the financial source I had negotiated with, meaning he wouldn't have to scurry around looking for a source of cash, things were made fairly easy for him. In effect, I provided him with a shotgun clause to use against me if he chose. Looking back, it appears extremely generous. At the time, though, I felt it would be a gesture and no more. Tom, I hoped, would recognize that the thirty-day period to make his decision about buying me out was not long enough to put everything in place. He would accept my offer, leave me sole owner, and move on to a new challenge. I was wrong.

Within a few days, Tom announced that he would buy my shares. I was stunned. Things had completely backfired on me. Now the company would be Tom's, and Tom's alone. It could grow and prosper without me. I would no longer be part of one of the great business success stories in Canadian history. I was devastated.

Later that day, Tom handed me a cheque and I found myself back on the street again. This time I had both a healthy bank account and the knowledge that I had helped create a substantial business from almost nothing. The first fact was comforting; the second was not.

"Money can't buy happiness" is a line we have heard through-out our lives, and I can assure you it's true. I had more money than I could have imagined ten years earlier. I was off the street, living in a luxury condo with a closet full of expensive clothes, and owned a private airplane. Neither money nor my drinking habit was a problem. On the brink of turning forty, my biggest challenge was to restore a sense of self-worth and find a way to be happy again.

I set out to enjoy my wealth. I furnished my condo, expanded my wardrobe, bought a new Mercedes-Benz, took my mother; Sean; Sean's wife, Michèle; and my sister, Maureen, on a Christmas vacation in Florida, and launched the holding company Kilrush Corporation (named for the county in Ireland where my father's family comes from) to invest in new business ventures. I planned to build Kilrush into a financial powerhouse with enough clout to someday eclipse Second Cup.

None of my possessions made me feel better. The condo grew claustrophobic, the holding company produced few initial successes, and driving around town in my new car wasn't much fun because wherever I went I passed a Second Cup outlet. Each was a reminder that part of my life—the most successful part so far—had ended, and I found myself taking long detours or choosing elaborate routes just to avoid encountering a Second Cup. But, thanks in part to my own franchising efforts, there were so many locations that they were almost impossible to avoid.

As time passed, I grew more resentful and jealous. My feel-ings were especially bitter because I was the guy who had started this particular ball rolling, and it had rolled right back over me.

My anger deepened when I realized that I had been mistaken about Tom's business abilities. I thought I was the one best suited to be Second Cup's CEO, but within a few months of my departure Tom appeared to be running things with great success. Besides understanding retailing better than I did, he was taking measured risks to build the business in the same entrepreneurial spirit I had planned to, and doing it brilliantly. With help from my brother Sean, who moved from vice-president in charge of leasing to assume my role as director of franchising, Tom launched a new expansion policy, a step necessitated by the company's heavy debt load assumed when Tom bought my shares, and it was paying off with enormous new growth.

Was I envious? Damn right. And a lot of other qualities that are not at all admirable. I had lost my status, my identity, and my means of measuring how far I had come from the street. One week I was Frank O'Dea, senior executive and co-founder of Second Cup. The next week I was Frank O'Dea, full stop. Who really gave a damn about me now? I had traded my identity for a whole bunch of figures on a bank statement. There is much comfort for the soul in calculating your achievements in life, and I was surprised to learn that the size of my bank account was a poor substitute for a positive identity.

I spent the next six months under a cloud of my own creation—six months of being driven by feelings of jealousy, rage, envy, all the classic self-destructive emotions. I had achieved so much, going from a penniless life on the streets to a guy wheeling a Mercedes in and out of his condo garage, yet I still felt denied. Denied what? Satisfaction? Stature? Recognition? I didn't know. But I needed to find out, and fix it.

Flying continued to be a liberating experience, and I spent a portion of my Second Cup profits on a new twin-engine airplane. I flew it as often as possible, searching for happiness in an open blue sky. Back on the ground, however, the darkness enveloped me again. I couldn't stay aloft forever. I had to find a solution that did not require wings and a propeller.

When nothing seemed to work, when I remained mired in this pit of rage and despair, I turned to prayer as a means of getting back in touch with my spirituality. This failed to boost my mood, but the act of prayer gave me the idea of isolating myself for a while. Perhaps solitary meditation would help me focus on the core of whatever was bothering me.

While participating in a self-help group several years earlier, I had visited a Jesuit retreat. Located just east of Toronto, Manresa was situated on a two-hundred-hectare estate once owned by two English earls, who had used it as their private hunting grounds. During the Second World War, the land was donated to the Jesuits, who created a spiritual renewal centre that included walking trails through pleasant woods and a meandering creek where salmon could be seen migrating upstream in September and October. As you might expect, accommodation was kept austere. Each room consisted of a bed, desk, chair, and little else. There were no locks on the doors, no radio or television, no magazines or newspapers. Meals were served and eaten in silence.

I wasn't solving my problems driving around the city in my spiffy new car, hanging out in my condo, or flying my airplane. More than staying active—usually by travelling in circles— I needed to cease moving, to remain at rest and let the world spin without me for a while. I needed to do this alone. Perhaps then I would discover a new direction. Manresa seemed the ideal place to do it.

The soft-spoken man who answered the phone identified himself as Father Bill. I explained my situation to him. I needed to deal with an event in my life that was causing me pain, I told him. I needed to purge myself of all the acidic emotions I was experiencing. I needed to feel good again.

Each of us encounters unforgettable people in our lives, men or women whose good sense and personal concern make a positive impact, and whose wisdom remains with us forever. In my life, Father Bill was one of them. A classic Jesuit, he possessed both an alphabet of university degrees and a first-class mind to apply his knowledge in practical ways, yet he lacked the sternness often attributed to Jesuits. He wrapped his inner strength and immense wisdom in a warm personality that was quick to respond to the deepest distress with an enlightening and often humorous observation. He was a compact man, and with his thick snow-white hair, pink cheeks, blue eyes, and casual dress, he looked as though he had been sent over from Central Casting to play a stereotypical priest in a Bing Crosby movie. But there was nothing artificial about Father Bill; he was the real thing.

During one of our conversations, Father Bill suggested looking at life as though it were a stained-glass window, with images created from a variety of colours, and each section of the window catching and reflecting the sun's rays. "If you were to enter a scene in the window," he said, "you might find yourself in a blue area. We all find ourselves in blue areas from time to time.

But if we keep moving, the blue eventually changes, perhaps first to cool green and then to warmer yellow. Eventually, we might find ourselves bathed in orange or red, which is the nicest place of all."

Just as likely, of course, we could find ourselves entering a blue area again. "But if you do," Father Bill explained, "it doesn't mean you're back in the same blue area where you began. It just means you're in a different place in the window, and if you keep moving you'll find yourself in a new yellow and red area."

Whether he was offering his views on simple or complex issues, he always distilled his ideas to a level I could understand. I have never forgotten his analogy of the stained-glass window, and I have used it many times since to reassure myself that a blue period is temporary, that I need to keep moving forward and find the orange and the red that I know is there, somewhere in the window.

This all came later. When I first telephoned seeking help, Father Bill suggested that I drive to Manresa the following Sunday and be prepared to spend the week in a silent retreat. During the day I would be free to stroll the grounds, but I must not communicate with anyone. In late afternoon, before the evening meal, Father Bill and I would chat about any topic I wanted.

Manresa proved to be as attractive as I remembered it. Entering the grounds that warm autumn day, I felt I had made a wise decision, a feeling that grew even stronger when I met Father Bill. "I make no promises to you," he said. "The objective for both of us is for you to drive out of here on Friday at peace."

The week began with high hopes. On my walks and while I sat, alone, in the chapel, memories of my Catholic upbringing drifted back—the good memories. The comfort of a Mother Church wrapping me in her protective arms, the peace of quiet meditation, the bliss of leaving the world's madness behind, all these feelings had been residing within me, though I had kept them hidden for many years. Now they were free to emerge.

I loved the serenity of that first day. I sat by myself for hours, hearing nothing but the birds, feeling nothing but the warm sun and cooling breezes against my skin.

The positive mood didn't last long. By the second day, the silence was getting to me. I began swinging back and forth between elation at dealing with my problem and despair that nothing was happening and that nothing *could* happen if I continued to isolate myself. Now I know that this feeling of rest-lessness always comes before the moment of discovery. I didn't realize it at the time, but I was getting ready to *hear* the change I would be making. I simply felt uneasy, and when I described my feelings to Father Bill, he assured me that my reactions were normal.

His assurance failed to register with me, and I began to suspect that each day spent in silence was another day of achiev-ing nothing. By noon on Wednesday, I felt I would go insane if I remained another day. I had to leave. I could see my car sitting in the parking lot, waiting for me. All I needed to do was climb in, start the engine, and in half an hour I'd be back in the city. I vowed to leave Manresa that evening and find a different way to deal with my problem.

I couldn't leave without saying goodbye to Father Bill, and giving him an explanation. At our meeting that afternoon, I explained my feelings of frustration, thanked him for his efforts, and announced that I would be departing that evening to look for some other solution.

Father Bill listened with empathy, as I knew he would. Then he said: "I'm going to make a suggestion to you. I think you're mad at God."

Mad at God? It took a while to understand what he meant. Through my childhood and right up to the point where I became sober, I retained the sense of an ecclesiastical God who exerted all the power and glory attributed to Him in the Bible. This is the One I prayed to, the One I relied upon to guide me when I needed help. I had often prayed to God in the darkest moments of my life on the streets and found comfort in my prayers.

But when I stopped drinking, my concept changed. Now I believed in a Higher Power, which was not the same as believing in the God of the Old or New Testament. So I couldn't understand the idea of being mad at it. Or Him.

We discussed this for a few minutes, then Father Bill asked what I would have done, while at Second Cup, if a supplier had let me down with a late delivery or a poor-quality product. "I would have picked up the telephone and talked to him," I said. "I would have let him know he had failed me, and that I was angry and disappointed."

"God doesn't have a telephone that I know of," Father Bill smiled. "But you can always write him a letter."

No matter how depressed I might have been about my situation, I remained in awe of Father Bill. His thinking was the most concise and lucid of any person I had ever met, or have met since for that matter. So I listened and took his advice. We agreed that I would stay the night and, at some point, write God a letter. If my feelings had not changed by morning, I would leave Manresa. What could I lose?

Returning to my room after the evening meal, I picked up a pen, placed a sheet of paper in front of me, and wrote: *Dear God. I prayed for this, and I got that. I think I got screwed. Yours truly.* Not exactly Paul's epistle to the Philippians, but in the process of scribbling these few words, something flowed out of me. Father Bill, I suppose, might have said I was moving from a blue piece of glass toward an orange one. In any case, after writing the note—it was too brief to call a letter—I walked around the grounds, enjoying the beautiful autumn evening. Then I returned to my room, climbed into bed, and fell asleep almost immediately.

I woke around three in the morning and, without thinking, reached for my note to God. Below the few sentences I had written a few hours earlier, I scribbled, *Do you trust me? Do you trust me?* Then I fell back asleep.

As I absorbed those words, I remembered that I had come from the darkest, most hopeless corner of skid row to achieve wealth and success beyond anything I could have imagined. If I had done it with the assistance of a Higher Power, whatever or whomever he might be, then I could trust him to help me in the future as well. I had no reason to fear failure, or doubt myself, or feel any sense of loss or resentment. No matter what has happened in my life since then, no matter what kind of anxiousness or emotional turmoil I'm going through, those words return: *Do you trust me?*

When confused in life, simply do the next right thing in front of you. I always knew what the next right thing to do was, but there were times when I chose not to do it, and I did something else instead. That was always a mistake.

I remained at Manresa to the end of the week, of course. Each time we met, Father Bill and I discussed what had happened, and how I could best apply the lesson in my life. We dealt with the betrayal I felt from not being associated with Second Cup, and the more we talked, the more my absence from the company was no longer of importance to me. I had moved out of the blue glass. I was in a warm, red place.

On Friday, I drove away from Manresa at peace with myself. I had met Father Bill's objective. Before I got into my car, Father Bill approached me, gripped my arm, and smiled. "Whenever you think about Second Cup," he said, "always remember that a Picasso is always a Picasso, no matter who owns it."

And the pain of losing Second Cup went away.

NINE

Taking Care
of Business

My original concept of Kilrush Corporation, the enterprise I
launched after leaving Second Cup, was to build it into a multi-
faceted powerhouse in Canadian business circles. If I could establish Kilrush as a bigger, more impressive operation than Second
Cup, I would have nothing else to prove to myself or to the world.

The experience at Manresa dissolved much of that childish
ambition. Now I wanted to achieve success for more rational
reasons. I wanted to build security for myself and opportunity for
others. I wanted to partner with clever, ambitious people to share
their dreams and help make them come true. I wanted to satisfy
the entrepreneurial spirit in me that extended back to the stories
I had read about William Zeckendorf.

Thank goodness I knew about Zeckendorf's various failures,
because the first few ventures by Kilrush did not exactly achieve

grand success. All I collected from them was experience, and experience, as someone said, is what you get when you were expecting something else. I had expected to make a million dollars. Instead, I lost about a million in ventures that were brilliant ideas but, like early Wright brothers airplanes, never really got off the ground.

About a year after my retreat at Manresa, I met a remarkable man named Scott Smith. In the mid-1980s, Scott learned of a company in Calgary providing mobile document-shredding services. Large companies, especially service firms such as banks and utilities, were being overwhelmed with the problem of storing massive volumes of documents well beyond the necessary retention period. Warehouses were overflowing with stacks of files that could not easily be discarded; they had to be shredded or incinerated—and few companies had the facilities to do either in large volume. Unless staff travelled with the records to a disposal site and watched them being destroyed, companies could never be certain that confidential data wouldn't find its way into the wrong hands, generating enormous legal and public relations problems.

Instead of taking the documents to the shredder, the Calgary firm's concept was to bring the shredder to the documents, parking it outside the client's door, where the disposal could be confirmed. Scott was so impressed with the idea that he travelled to Calgary and talked the company into giving him a job. The real market for paper shredding, Scott knew, was not in Calgary but Toronto, where most of the large corporate head offices were located—especially those of banks and investment firms. He persuaded his Calgary employer to set up operations in Toronto, with him as manager. After some time, however, Scott decided that the Calgary firm would not be capable of developing the industry effectively, and he bowed out shortly before the firm sank beneath the waves.

Scott knew how to correct the Calgary firm's errors, and he approached me as a source of venture capital, through Kilrush. I agreed with the prospects for a company that could solve corporate shredding needs and Kilrush advanced him $30,000 to buy a vehicle equipped with a large-volume shredder. We formed a partnership in the new company, which we christened Proshred Security, the world's first fully professional mobile document shredding system.

We bought a box van, and Scott and a neighbour installed a hammer shredder in the back. The shredder was exactly what its names implies. The thing pounded the paper rather than slicing it into strips like desktop shredders do. Unfortunately, the machine pounded more than paper. In operation, the shredder shook the truck so much that the vehicle looked like it was suffering from palsy. The Richter-scale pulsations of the shredder actually knocked parts off the van. And the noise sounded like a hundred tom-tom drummers practising in an airport hangar.

In fact, the noise and the shredder's primitive design led to a somewhat humorous event soon after the company's launch. Among our first customers was Bell Canada, which had many years' worth of statements, correspondence, and other documents to be shredded at its large downtown Toronto office. Our operator dutifully arrived at the site, moved the crates of documents into the truck and, after donning a set of earplugs to protect his hearing, started up the shredder.

The noisy machine drove the shredder with hydraulic fluid and, as with any hydraulic system, long periods of operation raised the temperature of the fluid. In the past, the hot hydraulic fluid had smoked a bit, but the machine had never operated long enough for the fluid to become as hot as it did this day. Soon great grey clouds of smoke were billowing out the back of the truck.

The operator, his ears snugly muffled against the noise and his attention focused on the job, continued feeding the shredder from inside the truck even as a nearby smoke alarm sounded, triggering a call to the fire department and setting off other alarms throughout the building. Within minutes, hundreds of employees stood outside watching as a hook-and-ladder, two pumper trucks, a couple of dozen firefighters, and a fleet of police cars arrived, along with TV news crews and other reporters. The firefighters gathered at the rear of the vehicle, prepared to inundate it with water and flame-retardant chemicals, when our operator emerged from the truck to find a mob of horrified spectators staring back at him. After that incident, we knew we had to find a better way of turning paper into confetti.

We found our solution practically in our own backyard, or at least within a hundred kilometres of it. A company in Cambridge, Ontario, run by a brilliant man named John Bell, had been developing shredders for disposal applications all over the world. John and his team quickly assessed our needs and developed a shredding system for us that became the industry standard for the next fifteen years. Based on a process designed to shred automobile tires, it worked well.

By the summer of 1987, we had perfected the shredders and were ready to install them in a fleet of trucks. We needed more capital, however, which meant approaching friends, business associates, and the usual financiers, most of whom listened to our proposal before shaking their heads and saying, "Don't you know that personal desktop computers are going to produce a paperless society? No one is going to need large-volume paper shredders because no one is going to be producing hard-copy documents."

This wasn't true, as we know now. Instead of producing paperless offices, PCs were generating enormous quantities of printed material compared with the large mainframe computers. More people could print more copies of more documents than ever before, and they did. When they weren't happy with the document's appearance or content, they made changes and hit the print button again—and again and again. Instead of a paperless environment, we were drowning in reams of the stuff, much of it containing confidential information.

Disposing of this material was a growing headache for corporations, hospitals, doctors' offices, government agencies, political organizations, and anyone else whose correspondence and records were confidential. Record storage companies were offering to destroy this material, but they brought little assurance that the documents would never see the light of day again. Many organizations were watching bales of files be carried off for disposal, only to have them be discovered a few days later in Dumpsters or scattered through a back alley. Hospitals were learning that patient records destined for incineration were blowing off garbage trucks and landing in gutters or on suburban lawns. Financial and taxation papers were getting into the hands of fraudsters, embezzlers, common thieves, and anyone else who could use the data to enrich themselves at the expense of others. Paper records generated years ago and sitting in warehouses weren't the chief concern; it was correspondence, reports, receipts, transaction records, and other data generated last week or last month.

We launched an aggressive marketing campaign that targeted anyone with substantial volumes of documents to destroy. "Watch your most confidential documents be destroyed at your doorstep," was our sales pitch, an appeal convincing enough to sign dozens of companies to long-term contracts.

We introduced innovative ideas that helped develop the company quickly. Fast expansion was essential, I knew, because our service could be easily copied—and, as things turned out, it was. Our plan was to grow fast enough to offer wider services, enjoy the economic benefits of scale and volume, and stay ahead of the competition as long as possible.

Much of our success was due to our ability to provide first-rate service and guaranteed security for customers. A good deal of the professional management expertise came from my brother Sean, who left Second Cup within two years of my departure and joined me at Proshred.

Proshred did well also because it shared an important quality with Second Cup. Like the coffee operation, Proshred represented not just a new company but the advent of a new industry. That's a significant distinction, and it brings with it both advantages and disadvantages. One of the main advantages is a lack of competition, leaving you free to innovate and price your services according to demand—for innovators of new services, margins are high and opportunities unlimited. The disadvantage is that pioneers in business face the same challenges as pioneers in a new country. They must overcome challenges all on their own, while educating customers first about the need and then about the solution. In effect, they blaze the trail for competition to come roaring in along a marked path. The competition, when it arrives, builds on the pioneer's work, avoids its errors, and usually brings sufficient capital to squeeze the pioneer aside.

As pioneers of the mobile shredder industry, we expected other companies to fit the pattern, arriving to compete with greater clout, deeper pockets, and a proven model—Proshred. That's exactly what happened. After buying Scott's share of Proshred in 1992, Sean and I operated the company for ten years. By then, several competitors were vying with us for business and we faced a decision to either stay and fight or cash in our chips and go home. We cashed in the chips. Proshred remains a player in the industry, having expanded throughout North America. Whenever I hear another story of its enormous success, I smile at the memory of that van shaking at the curb as though two elephants were doing the rhumba inside it, and the puzzled operator emerging from a cloud of smoke wearing his noise-silencing earplugs to face an army of disaster workers and spectators.

NOT ALL MY BUSINESS VENTURES SUCCEEDED, but that's the nature of exploring new ideas and taking risks. Free of Second

Cup, both emotionally and monetarily, I discovered a knack for evaluating and nurturing new ideas, profiting when they blossomed, and harvesting wisdom when they withered. I learned something from every success and every failure I achieved over the years. Sometimes, the most valuable lessons emerged from the failures.

Vidiwall was a good example. By purchasing rights to use this technology, I could install sixty-eight- or eighty-centimetre LED video screens to fill a large wall area in a shopping mall. The screens would project a montage of messages, create one massive visual filling the entire wall, or use combinations of large and small visuals simultaneously. The Vidiwalls would alternate between entertaining scenes of skiing, sailing, or other colourful activities and video advertisements. We envisioned hundreds of Vidiwalls linked to a central computer facility, creating a coast-to-coast network.

The market potential for Vidiwall seemed enormous. Imagine a chain retailer like The Gap or Peoples Jewellers being able to display a new product or special pricing in every mall where their stores are found, changing the message daily or even hourly, all the while directing shoppers to check out the deals for themselves.

The idea was sound and the potential was enormous. So why didn't it work? The project was ahead of its time. Also, every business idea needs a champion, someone who brings ability, enthusiasm, contacts, vision, all those entrepreneurial qualities, to the job. And this one didn't have it. We didn't have the right guy to make it work. The fellow who approached me with the idea wasn't the person to ensure its success, and I couldn't find anyone else to launch and manage it. Vidiwall proved an expensive lesson, but most lessons in business tend to carry a big price tag.

While getting over the failure of Vidiwall, I encountered Greig Clarke, a smart buttoned-down kind of guy who had created College Pro Painters. Greig suggested we create a venture capital fund to provide cash for promising start-up operations. He and I, along with other carefully selected board members, would monitor the companies we invested in and, if we felt it necessary, step in and put the operations back on track.

We raised the money, recruited a first-rate board of directors, and launched the Horatio Fund as a holding company. The fund didn't bat .1000, but it scored a few winners, including ARXX Walls and Foundations, a building-products company with contract manufacturing throughout North America, which produces insulated concrete forms. This building technique uses insulated concrete blocks to construct foundations or entire structures. The savings in construction costs and, later, in energy, are real. In fact, I recently built a major extension on my house using ARXX products.

ARXX, to the best of my knowledge, is one of the largest and most successful of about seventy similar companies in North America, but it didn't get to that position without a lot of hard work and diligence. As major investors, we had to change management from time to time. During one of these shakeups, I became chairman of the board and Greig became CEO. When Greig chose to step down as CEO, I took his place, a decision that requires me to commute between my home in Ottawa and ARXX's head office in Cobourg, Ontario. Despite these recent hiccups, the company looks like it will be a winner, and I'm proud to play a role in its success.

Another project for which I had great hopes was Samaritan Air Service, whose dedicated aircraft had sophisticated on-board diagnostic and treatment equipment, invaluable for critically ill patients. Adam Keller brought me the idea, and it was a good one. Until we created Samaritan, transporting patients by air meant removing a couple of seats from a chartered airplane, sliding a cot in their place, and taking off.

With Samaritan, we converted a fleet of MV2s into flying ambulances complete with heart machines, oxygen generators, and trauma facilities, plus qualified personnel to ensure that the patient received full medical attention during the flight. The response was good, and although our primary market was aging Canadian snowbirds vacationing in Florida, our aircraft were employed to bring home patients from as far away as Brazil.

The economics were in our favour, especially for the snow-bird market. While the vast majority of Canadians who venture to Florida and points south for the winter buy medical insurance, the insurance coverage is provided by Canadian and international companies. Should a vacationer suffer serious injuries or disease requiring extensive medical treatment and a long-term hospital stay, insurers want to return the patient to Canada, where this country's medical health service will assume the treatment costs. With hospital stays in the south-ern United States costing $2000 a day or more, the expense to transport patients back into the bosom of Canadian medical care is a comparative bargain.

So the need was there, and Samaritan filled that need well. Unfortunately, the company got caught in a Perfect Storm of problems, all of them beyond our control.

The first was weather. That autumn was especially mild, and the unusual mildness stretched through winter, encouraging Canadians to remain north longer. The sharp drop of the loonie against the U.S. dollar proved another incentive for Canadians to stay home. On top of this, many U.S. doctors and hospitals resisted early release of patients for travel back to Canada, recognizing that a patient treated in Canada was income lost. Finally, Ontario premier Mike Harris revved up his cost-cutting program, closing hospitals across the province and reducing the number of beds. The combination of a shrinking market, foreign resistance, and limited hospital openings was too much for Samaritan to handle, especially given its high overhead.

Not all my energies during this period were related to business. Shortly after the scandal erupted over Ben Johnson's use of steroids at the 1988 Olympics, I accepted an invitation to join the Canadian Olympic Association's committee on ethics. I was amazed to learn that no code of conduct existed for dealing with Olympic athletes and coaches. It took some investigation by me and the committee chair, Clint Ward, along with other committee members, to reveal a state of affairs that had been swept under the rug for years.

It became clear to all of us on the committee that the relationship between our Olympic athletes and their sponsors and coaches was subject to abuse. In some cases, it resembled a hostage situation, with sponsors and coaches controlling almost every aspect of the athletes' lives. Many athletes were faced with a choice that amounted to no choice at all: Either follow the commands of coaches and sponsors or abandon your dreams of being an Olympic competitor. These directives are not limited to regimens of training and conditioning, the usual role of coaches. They can include pressure to take performance-enhancing drugs and being subjected to sexual pressures from sponsors and coaches, an abuse suffered by both male and female competitors. No system existed to protect the athletes.

The committee grew determined to stop this, and over a number of meetings we drew up a code of conduct and values that enabled athletes to blow the whistle on unacceptable behaviour by coaches and sponsors without jeopardizing their careers. After drafting the final version, the other committee members and I travelled to St. John's, Newfoundland, where we submitted the code to a meeting of the Olympic Association. I am proud to say that the code was accepted by the association, and it has morphed into a system of values that have played a prominent role in the activities of the Canadian Olympic Association ever since.

On a brighter note, my involvement in the Olympic Movement introduced me to a wonderful woman named Carol Anne Letheren, president of the Canadian Olympic Association, who recommended me as a board member to The Mount Pleasant Group, a trust that manages several cemeteries in Toronto. The Group's origins date back to the 1820s, when the only two cemeteries in town were Anglican and Roman Catholic; if you were neither of those faiths, there was no burial place for you. In an act of Christian charity, a few wealthy families contributed money to the community to purchase a potter's field at what is now the northwest corner of Bloor and Yonge streets. This marked the beginning of a non-denominational approach to cemeteries in Toronto and, as years passed, Mount Pleasant Cemetery and other properties were created under the trust's umbrella. (An interesting historical note: The first recording secretary of The Mount Pleasant Group was William Lyon Mackenzie, who became Toronto's first mayor and went on to lead a rebellion in Upper Canada, barely escaping the noose for his actions. The current group is not nearly so seditious.)

Of the many people I have been fortunate to meet and work with over the years, none exceeds Carol Anne Letheren for her ability, dedication, and warmth, which made her sudden death in February 2001 exceptionally tragic. I still miss her, as does everyone who knew and admired her.

I joined The Mount Pleasant Group after a decision had been made to launch a new kind of funeral service. Rightly or wrongly, the public believed that many conventional funeral homes took advantage of bereaved families during a vulnerable period. Was there a better way of providing the features that the grieving families wanted, while avoiding costly excesses?

The solution was The Simple Alternative, or TSA, to be operated by The Mount Pleasant Group. TSA would offer cremation facilities and auxiliary support service at a price much lower than some of the more extravagant packages a few funeral homes were promoting. The Ontario government deemed TSA a funeral home. In Ontario, cemeteries are not permitted to run funeral homes, so The Mount Pleasant Group established an independent board to coordinate the operation. This was essentially a start-up operation, and my experience in that area was deemed valuable enough for me to be invited to join the board.

The years I spent serving on The Mount Pleasant Group's TSA board opened my eyes to several weighty facts. One was that the most important decision concerns the composition of the board itself. The capability of the people who sit on the board and the values they bring to the table are the driving force behind the board's effectiveness and the quality of its decisions. Board members must share similar values in order to reach meaningful decisions and function at an acceptable level of harmony and efficiency. It's not just a matter of assembling a range of skill sets, as though gathering the ingredients for a cake. Compatibility among the members is essential, regardless of their individual talents.

I found the Mount Pleasant board exceptional in this regard, and it has achieved outstanding results. Many infamous corporate shenanigans in recent years can be traced directly back to directors whose values were not shared, were frequently in opposition to other board members, or were subjugated to the wishes of a domineering chairperson. This may have generated colourful and dramatic board meetings but it rarely, if ever, served the corporation well. In the United States, the Sarbanes-Oxley Act of 1992 introduced rules designed to ensure good governance, and many businesspeople consider the act draconian in its impact. My sense is that Sarbanes-Oxley tried to solve the problem with rules when it is far easier and far more effective to address the issues by selecting the right people to sit on a corporate board. Matching the values of board members to the values of the corporation is invariably preferable, in my view, to imposing rule of individual and collective responsibility, and the most successful boards of directors have known and applied these guidelines for years.

The other lesson I learned from my experience with The Mount Pleasant Group involved the issue of governance. Every board of directors is, or should be, aware of the implications of its decisions and their effects on those beyond the boardroom. The Mount Pleasant Group is reminded of this in ways that most corporations could never comprehend. When you purchase a burial plot, the cemetery management assumes responsibility for maintaining that plot in perpetuity. Gravesites in Mount Pleasant cemetery, purchased for ten or fifteen dollars back in the 1850s, have been maintained all the years since and will continue to be maintained in the future. The awareness that decisions you make today may have an effect two or three hundred years from now is a sobering thought to board members; it ensures that these decisions are reached only after much consideration.

Too many corporate decisions, it seems to me, are made with a dramatically different time frame in mind. Some corporations refuse to focus beyond the next quarterly financial statement. The Mount Pleasant Group looks a century into the future. I leave it to you to conclude which decisions are made with greater reflection and sobriety.

TEN

A Chapter
for Nancy

While my business life was successful, my personal life remained somewhat chaotic. I drifted through relationships, diverting my sense of failure in that corner of my life with a good deal of volunteer work.

One of the projects I supported was a prominent self-help group, and in the late 1980s, I chaired the organizing committee during the group's annual conference. The committee was made up of members of the self-help group as well as partners and friends of alcoholics. Among the committee members at these sessions, one woman stood out. She represented spouses and friends of people with alcohol problems, and her intelligence, her sense of humour, her casual elegance, and yes, doggone it, her beauty were remarkable. Her name was Nancy, and while she projected a bright and positive personality, I was completely unaware that she was dealing with some personal problems.

In time, I learned that Nancy was married to a verbally abusive man, one who seemed intent on destroying their marriage in the same way he had destroyed his previous two. Raised a Catholic, Nancy clung to her faith despite her husband's brutal attacks. "Why do you insist on attending Mass?" he would bait her. "It's a stupid waste of time. If your God is so great, why are there wars and diseases? Why do innocent people suffer? Why do you insist on making a fool of yourself?"

There were other attacks as well, often far more vicious and cruel. Nancy told me that she felt like a crumbling porcelain doll during this period. "Pieces of my personality would be broken off," she explained, "and I would just get one glued back in place when another would fall away."

Over the next couple of years, we saw each other at committee meetings or social events hosted by mutual friends. I admired her from afar without becoming involved in her life. Until 1990, when she told me she had left her husband. As inevitable and necessary as the marriage failure may have been, the pain it caused her was evident in her eyes. We began having coffee together, which led to lunches and tennis games. Despite her melancholy, Nancy made me laugh, something few people had achieved at that point in my life.

Still, her husband's abuse had taken its toll. While I had emerged from my experience at Manresa with strengthened faith, Nancy had escaped her marriage with a shaken belief. Being the stronger partner in a relationship was unfamiliar to me, but the role of spiritual anchor was one I enjoyed.

Although Nancy's husband, insufferable to the end, refused to grant her a divorce after they separated, Nancy set out to start her life anew. She moved into an apartment near my condo, and we were soon seeing a good deal of each other. She became "the girl next door" to me, literally and, in her natural, unspoiled outlook, figuratively as well.

It soon became apparent that we were the source of each other's happiness and strength, and I suppose I should have basked in the warm glow. But I didn't. More precisely, I couldn't. Some people cannot handle success. I couldn't handle happiness.

I backed away from any hint that we were part of something permanent and special, something we all seek in our lives yet not everyone discovers. After every high point, every occasion when both of us recognized how fortunate we were to find each other, I would withdraw and discover reasons not to see her for a while.

I remained in therapy, which was helping me deal with some issues, though not the ones associated with Nancy and me. Once, when I began performing my dance of pulling away, Nancy asked where I thought we were going with our relationship.

"Relationship?" I countered. "We don't have a relationship."

Instead of exploding in anger or bursting into tears, Nancy laughed. "What do you mean?" she said. "We've been seeing each other all this time and you claim it's not a relationship?"

I replied that time alone does not define a relationship.

"You have been seeing your therapist for about three years now," she countered. "Doesn't that qualify as a relationship?"

No, I responded. That's not a relationship. Relationships only develop between two people with intentions to marry, neatly discounting all the other relationships I had experienced in my life—with family, with politicians, with businesspeople.

Nancy couldn't fathom my logic. Nor, with the perspective of time, can I. Now, of course, I realize that I was afraid of experiencing happiness. We drifted like this for about a year, with me moving closer and closer to her—until I pulled away again, having decided I didn't deserve all this happiness.

One day, Nancy announced that her employer had offered her a promotion, one that would mean relocating to Vancouver. Driven in part by her natural ambition and in part by her exasperation with my inability to admit that we were even in a relationship, she accepted the job. I remained stoic at the news. Perhaps, I reasoned, this was best for both of us. She could find happiness somewhere else, and I would no longer be frightened by the threat of being happy.

On the day she left Toronto, I drove her to the airport, promised that if I ever had reason to visit Vancouver I would look her up, gave her a quick kiss, and left her standing there among her dozen or so pieces of luggage. It definitely was not Bogart and Bergman in the goodbye scene from *Casablanca*.

My coolness lasted a day or two and was followed by a succession of telephone calls and trips to Vancouver. I helped her find an apartment, shopped for furnishings, and celebrated Christmas with her. I enjoyed her presence and soon realized how much I needed her. This attachment grew more significant when we were unexpectedly faced with imminent parenthood. The news both delighted and dismayed us. We wanted to marry, but Nancy's husband continued to refuse her a divorce, and Nancy began the long legal process to extricate her from her marriage.

After about a year in Vancouver—Nancy couldn't handle the city's grey skies and rainy days—she left her job to return east. We settled in Oakville, where Nancy and I built a home for the family we planned. Our beautiful daughter, Taylor, soon arrived, along with advice from Nancy's physician. "If you want more children," he told her, "you'd better have them soon." Entering her forties, Nancy was facing the realities imposed by the legendary biological clock. Taylor was followed fourteen months later by her sister, Morgan. Nancy's divorce was finally granted, and we married at our home in Oakville in 1995.

Marriage and fatherhood so late in life was a revelation for me. Every parent knows—or soon learns—that children drive the family's agenda, but accepting this proved a challenge at times. The question "What have I gotten myself into?" popped into my head often when the children were young, though I doubt if it occurred any more frequently to me at fifty than it does to parents at forty, thirty, or twenty. The rewards of parenthood justify the challenges.

Describing one's spouse as "the best thing that ever happened to me" is perhaps the ultimate romantic cliché, but a cliché is a cliché because it is true. My decision to stop drinking and get off the street, to learn to trust God on that dark night at Manresa, and all the satisfaction of my successful business decisions does not measure up to the multiple ways in which Nancy has brightened and enriched my life.

Very early in our relationship, I recognized Nancy's amazing intuitive ability, her capacity to see beneath the surface of people and events. You can't fool this woman: She senses things, especially where our children are concerned, that totally escape me, flying both under my radar and over my head.

Nancy and I are very different yet very compatible, and I suspect that each supports the other. Nancy still has friends from her youngest years of childhood. My friends, in comparison, are from various events and periods in my adult life. Among the ways in which our values coincide is our mutual dedication to performing volunteer work. We are committed to finding ways of improving the world, not just for ourselves and our children but for those distant from us, the distance measured in socio-economic and cultural terms as well as in kilometres.

We have also reversed roles. In the beginning, I was Nancy's anchor. I provided the solid foundation while she recovered from the emotional bruising of her marriage. Now she is my anchor. Whenever dark moods begin to envelop me, whenever I suspect that I am a fraud managing to convince a gullible world that I am worthy of its love and respect, I turn to Nancy for assurance and always find it.

ELEVEN

Somebody Must Care for the Children

To say that things turned around for me after Manresa is something of an understatement. Kept busy with ventures that were both fun and profitable, I was amazed at how my life had improved. A part of me might have been content to coast toward the far horizon, pleased and content. Instead, I encountered yet another of those nudges that send me into new, unexpected directions. This one, unlike the others, had global implications.

During his too-few years on earth, a friend named Sean O'Sullivan accomplished goals that most people could not achieve in several lifetimes. In 1972, at age twenty, Sean was elected the youngest member of Parliament in Canadian history. It was no fluke; he displayed a level of intelligence, drive, and charisma that could easily have eclipsed that of Pierre Trudeau. (Sean was a dedicated Conservative, so a match between the two would have been fascinating to watch.) Those who met him felt they had never seen so many key qualities assembled with such balance and power in a single person before, and everyone believed it was only a matter of time before he took the first step up a ladder that would surely place him in the prime minister's office.

His supporters watched his progress for about five years. Then, Sean stunned the nation by announcing he was resigning from politics to enter the priesthood, where he could better fulfill his personal dedication to public service. Parliament's loss, many people consoled themselves, was God's gain.

Ordained in 1981 and immediately appointed director of vocations for the Archdiocese of Toronto, Father Sean was poised to play a major role in the Catholic Church, ready and able to achieve any ambition he might set for himself. Then, in case we needed proof that life can be unfair and much of its unfairness is beyond our understanding, Sean was diagnosed with leukemia. He refused to surrender to the disease, which was not surprising to those who knew him well. In the time left to him, he wrote his autobiography, *Both My Houses: Politics to Priesthood*, and served as a publisher of *The Catholic Register*.

Despite the limits imposed by his disease, Father Sean still wasn't finished. In 1987, the year he was named Companion of the Order of Canada, Father Sean prepared an important document on the plight of the elderly and disabled for the Government of Ontario, an assessment that improved life for these disadvantaged citizens in a way no single study has done, before or since.

When I met Father Sean, I had been first captivated by his intelligence, ambition, and humour; then devastated by news of his disease; and, finally, inspired by his courage and determination in the face of death. We stayed in touch and, in 1988, Father Sean invited me to join him in Florida for a few days, where he was escaping the Canadian winter. I set off, looking forward to some rest and relaxation in Father Sean's stimulating company.

Shortly after takeoff, I struck up a conversation with the traveller seated next to me, a tall, balding man who was joyfully unkempt in the manner of the TV detective Colombo. He was Peter Dalglish, employed by UNICEF to work with street kids in Sudan. That country's problems are not as recent as current news reports suggest: Twenty years ago, its challenges were as severe as they are today, and the situation of Sudanese children could only be described as appalling.

Thousands of homeless and abused children in Sudan had abandoned their villages to set out for the capital, Khartoum, where the prospects of employment and shelter seemed more promising. Now the city, Peter explained, was awash with kids who had no hope of obtaining a home, an education, or a job. Much of his time was spent seeking ways to improve the lives of the children, and on one particular occasion he achieved enormous success.

A few weeks earlier, Peter had visited the U.S. embassy in Khartoum looking for something to entertain the street children and help them forget, for a short time at least, their deplorable circumstances. The embassy could offer little, but looking through its film library, Peter found a reel of Tom and Jerry cartoons. This particular series, consisting of a conniving mouse outwitting a ferocious cat, contained little or no dialogue, so the language wouldn't be an issue. The children, Peter decided, would enjoy it.

Borrowing both the film and the embassy's projector, Peter ran the movie in the small building that served as his headquarters, projecting it against a plain white wall. "The children were mesmerized by the cartoons," Peter told me. "Absolutely mesmerized. They didn't understand English, but they didn't have to. The action was entirely visual. I watched children whom I had never seen smile burst into laughter. While the movie ran, they forgot about their plight. After I showed the entire reel, they begged to see it again, then asked me to run it the following night as well."

Word spread. Perhaps a dozen children watched the cartoons that first night. The second night, at least a hundred kids showed up, and the third night, over a thousand children—so many that Peter had to carry the projector outside, where the children squatted on the ground and laughed at the antics of a cartoon cat and mouse projected on a faded cotton sheet fastened to a mud-brick wall.

It was a heartwarming tale, until Peter told of a darker, chilling side. "Do you know," he said, "that the World Health Organization has found that 23 percent of street kids around the world are HIV-positive? Twenty-three percent!"

These children, Peter explained, were triply degraded. As street kids, with no guardians or welfare organizations to turn to, they were prey to sexual and economic abuse. As HIV sufferers without constant effective treatment, they were condemned to an early death. The same disease stigmatized them in the eyes of those with the means to provide the care the children so desperately needed, and so their plight was often ignored. This tragedy is multiplied to horrific levels: Peter told me that maybe as many as one hundred million children around the world lived on the street—most, but not all of them, in Africa and Asia.

Few people wanted to help these kids, not even to explain the dangers they faced from disease and predators, both the economic and the sexual kind. The only source of information the children trusted was themselves. "The street kids have a slogan," Peter said. "It's, 'My mother, the street.' The street, with all its dirt and dangers, protects and teaches them. That's what a mother does. That's what a mother should do. For them, it's the street."

Their mother, I learned, was less than perfect. The street might teach them how to beg for money, how to get their hands on food and clothing, and how to avoid abusive police and thugs, but it could not teach them about AIDS. Children barely into their teens were being assessed as HIV-positive. Shunned by society and devoid of even the most basic health care, what would become of them? Millions of children around the world needed to be taught about the disease. But how do you reach illiterate kids speaking a hundred different languages?

The solution, Peter and I decided somewhere over South Carolina, just might be an animated film, the same technology that depicted a rambunctious cat and a clever mouse romping about, and captured the attention of the children in Khartoum. Perhaps it could be used to educate as well as entertain. Why not create an animated film with a health message inside a storyline that would attract and hold the attention of street children while they learned of a fatal danger that the street could not teach them until it was too late? By changing the voice-over narration, it could be adapted for use in many countries and cultures at minimal expense.

It would all take time and money, of course, and more of both than would be needed today. Back in 1988, computer animation was not as sophisticated as it is now. Production costs for cartoons created via computers today are a fraction of those two decades ago. Making animated features involved drawing and photographing twenty-four images for every second of film time. A twenty-minute animated film required almost thirty thousand pictures, each rendered by an animation artist. Nobody that we knew of had used an animated film as a tool for educating street children. Yet, as Peter's experience with the Tom and Jerry features had proven, animation was an excellent way to reach these children.

If we were to succeed, the money would have to be found— lots of it.

By the time we landed in Florida, Peter and I had agreed that we would co-produce an animated film teaching street kids how to avoid AIDS. He was off to Sudan; I was looking forward to a few days of R and R. But my life, I recognized, was about to move in yet another direction.

Over the next few days in Florida, I found myself becoming more and more captivated with the idea of producing an animated film to teach street kids about AIDS. I had suffered abuse as a child. I had been older than most of these victims, and I had enjoyed a roof over my head and warm meals to satisfy my hunger, yet the pain of the abuse lingered. I had also lived in the street, as these children did, never daring to look beyond my next meal and my next place to sleep. Images of children, boys and girls, fending for themselves in the filthy gutters of Khartoum, Calcutta, São Paulo, and other cities, etched themselves in my mind. The children must be helped, and I knew no one more aware of the need for that help than myself. This, I decided, was a calling that I dared not ignore.

The idea gained greater strength during my conversations with Father Sean. His selfless dedication to making life better for the poor and oppressed of the world, even during the few months left to him, convinced me to follow through on the ideas Peter and I had discussed.

I said goodbye to Father Sean, there in the warmth of the sun, for the last time. He died soon after while undergoing a bone marrow transplant.

Back in Canada, Peter and I reconnected to create Street Kids International (SKI). Our initial objective was to produce and distribute an animated film explaining AIDS to homeless children, coordinating our efforts with similar organizations around the world. In time, it expanded in line with both a growing awareness of the plight of these children, and the growing number of children subject to horrific crimes and treatment.

The philosophy of SKI was and remains this: We believe that street youth have the potential for transforming their own lives when given non-judgmental support in developing skills, making choices, and accessing opportunities. We identified four broad categories of SKI's activities: Street Work Initiatives for business education, business start-up, and micro-credit for street youth; Street Health Initiatives to assist street youth to make informed choices related to sexual health and substance abuse;

Street Rights Initiatives that advocate the rights of street youth—their right to access health care, safe work opportunities, and education; and Street Talk, a series of audio conferences discussing issues that confront youth around the world. Recently, SKI launched Street Jibe. Unlike previous SKI programs, this one is directed toward Canadian youth, especially those suffering from poverty and homelessness.

In the beginning, our most pressing need was for funds to produce the animated film. We began by recruiting a board of directors, and I asked each to sign a guarantee for a bank loan of $30,000 for start-up capital. When they did, we were in business, but we still had no money for the film.

Peter contacted a long-time friend of his, a bright writer–producer named Chris Lowry, and the three of us visited Ottawa looking for production seed money. Our plan was to make a presentation to Jake Epp, the minister of health. When he couldn't see us, we were referred to his appointee on the subject of AIDS, Dr. Norbert Gilmore, a senior physician at Royal Victoria Hospital in Montreal. Nobody ever called Norbert by his full name, or even called him "Dr. Gilmore." To everyone who met and dealt with him, he was simply Nobby.

Nobby Gilmore responded to our idea with enthusiasm, a reassuring sign. AIDS was still viewed primarily as a disease affecting gay men, and much of the mainstream culture was expressing little interest in, or sympathy for, its sufferers. Nobby's reaction was heartening. When he asked what he could do for us, I went directly to the point: "We need money to get this film done."

With much encouragement and lots of valuable advice from Nobby, we raised more than $2 million to cover the production of an animated film that could be used to teach street children the dangers of AIDS and how to avoid it. Peter was responsible for amassing much of this funding, thanks to his international contacts and his unbridled passion for the idea. When people recognized its value and grew comfortable with the notion of supporting the film, the money began pouring in. Then the hard part began.

Our film would have to be world-class in production quality. The subject was too important, and the need too critical, to settle for little more than an extended TV commercial. We also needed a well-planned approach to the message, one that acknowledged certain realities. Because of the association of AIDS with gay culture, it was controversial, a common response from much of the public being "Serves them right!" Gay men and promiscuous women who contracted AIDS could count on little support and less sympathy from much of the straight population, even in a relatively tolerant country like Canada. It would be much worse, we knew, beyond our own borders.

If we were to succeed in placing copies of the film around the world, we would have to deal with this hostile attitude. We also needed to reduce the hostility of the gatekeepers, people in power who wanted no part of the crisis. They would, I sensed, assume that addressing the AIDS problem meant approving its cause, and thus prefer to do nothing at all.

Everyone in the film industry knows Canada produces some of the world's most gifted animators, and this was as true in 1989 as it is today. Ten years earlier, a Canadian animation producer won an Academy Award for his contribution to *Every Child*, produced by the National Film Board to mark 1979 as the United Nations' Year of the Child. *Every Child* went on to win the 1980 Oscar for Best Short Animated Film and was screened to enthusiastic audiences around the world. The film's producer and writer, Derek Lamb, was the guy we wanted for our movie, and we recruited him, along with animator Kai Pindal.

Early in our first session to outline the story, we realized the significant hurdle facing us. None of us had been a street kid in a Third World country, targeted by perverts and exploiters with virtually no support system to lean on. Peter was familiar with the appalling conditions of these children, of course, but we were the group assigned to communicate in a manner that the kids could grasp and respond to, and there we were, a bunch of white, middle-class Canadians sitting in a studio in Toronto, discussing how to reach illiterate children in Africa, Asia, and South America, kids whose only possessions were the ragged clothes on their backs. "Let's face it," somebody said at one point, "it can't be done. Not by us sitting here." Everyone agreed. Since we could not decide how to frame the message for the kids, we would rely on the kids to frame the message for us.

We had to start somewhere, and we began with a broad story-line illustrated by a series of drawings organized like newspaper comic strips. These storyboards depicted how the tale would unfold, and Derek and Kai set out with them to visit the slums of Khartoum and other Third World cities with a large population of street children. Kai would start things rolling by sketching caricatures of children on a drawing pad and handing them back to his subjects who, of course, were delighted. When several children had gathered, Derek would explain the film's story to the children through a translator. Then he would ask how believable it was and how much it addressed their concerns and experiences.

The children were rarely shy about expressing their opinions, even while Derek photographed them and Kai sketched them—their facial expressions, body language, clothing, gestures, and meagre possessions. They also volunteered their experiences, including how and by whom they were exploited. They told us who they trusted, and who they feared and avoided, and why.

Early in their research, Derek and Kai realized that kids everywhere were familiar with kung fu. Some of us would have preferred a less violent activity, but the children understood this martial art. It was a universal understanding, and it soon became central to our storyline.

Derek and Kai responded to suggestions from the children, shaping the storyline here, adding a new twist there, making this character more threatening and that one more believable. Then they carried the revised storyboard off to a new group of kids in a different city, building and fine-tuning the tale to broaden its appeal while honing its message.

Throughout this exercise, we kept looking beyond the film as the sole means of conveying our message. The movie's true potential, we recognized, could only be achieved if it launched a dialogue between the people presenting the film to the children and the children themselves. Only when the kids began interpreting and discussing the film on a broad scale would they begin to heed its message.

One step we took was quietly ingenious. Each time Derek and Kai returned from a session with the kids, they brought several rolls of film with them. Back in Canada, they processed the film and began taping these photographs to the wall of our meeting room—pictures of boys and girls sitting on crumbling curbs, sprawling on benches, splashing in water, swinging from tree limbs, and doing what millions of kids all over the world do, with one exception: These kids had no home to return to at the end of the day, no parent to hug and protect them, no fresh clothes to change into, and no snug bed to sleep in. Nevertheless, in every photo, most noticeable in the close-ups of their faces, the children were smiling at the camera.

Eventually, we had hundreds of these pictures on the wall, smiling at us as we continued to develop the animated film intended for them. Their faces reminded us of the goals we had set for ourselves, and the people who counted the most. We could not raise our eyes from the storyboards or the script without seeing those eyes shining with hope. I cannot think of a more effective motivator for us because I am convinced that none existed.

The children weren't the only audience whose views had to be accounted for. We needed to anticipate and either accommodate or deflect concerns and objections from the gatekeepers, those who would either promote or condemn our film according to their own agenda.

After reviewing and assembling all our material, we moved into production with a team of animators and sound effects people, working closely with the World Health Organization (WHO) and with valuable assistance from the National Film Board. Titled *Karate Kids*, the movie has a running time of twenty-three minutes. Besides being long enough to deliver a detailed message and short enough to retain the audience's attention, twenty-three minutes was the preferred film length for TV networks, which would insert seven minutes of commercials to yield a half-hour show.

The first animated film to teach children about serious health and safety issues, *Karate Kids* premiered in 1990 at a WHO meeting in Geneva. The meeting was attended by AIDS workers from several countries at the invitation of Jonathan Mann, who headed the WHO's Global Program on AIDS. (Tragically, Jonathan Mann and his wife died in the crash of Swissair Flight 111 off the coast of Nova Scotia in September 1998.) Many topics were on the agenda, most of them outlined on the prepared program. For that first public showing of *Karate Kids*, however, we asked that nothing be said about it. Jonathan Mann simply announced the film, the lights dimmed, and the projector began to roll.

When the lights came back up, Mann turned to us and proclaimed *Karate Kids* a remarkable film that would educate and save street children from one of the most serious health concerns of the twenty-first century. Subsequently, the WHO targeted forty million children to see *Karate Kids*. (Unfortunately, Kenya and the Philippines, two countries with exceptionally high numbers of street children and an AIDS problem of similar scope, banned *Karate Kids* solely because of its reference to condoms as a means of avoiding AIDS. Such are the challenges facing international agencies dedicated to assisting the weakest sectors of a nation's society.)

Producing the film wasn't the end of the process by any means. As we anticipated, we encountered resistance from various people in positions of power who asserted that communication of any kind on the subject of AIDS was unnecessary, unwarranted, or unwise, and probably all three. We evaded these people wherever possible, putting the film on screens and walls where kids could easily access it. When the gatekeepers said no to the film, we hijacked AIDS conferences; through the pressure of public opinion and sympathetic government representatives attending the sessions, the naysayers were forced to accept and use the film. When we met with resistance to the idea of educating street children about AIDS, we simply bypassed that person and approached someone more open-minded with the guts and power to arrange for the film's showing. We also began to train workshop leaders, people whose job was to be present when *Karate Kids* was shown to the children and discuss its message and implications with them.

Karate Kids was so well received that SKI launched a second film project dealing with substance abuse among street children. Titled *Goldtooth*, it featured characters from *Karate Kids*. Its title is derived from the villain, Mr. Goldtooth, who encourages children to start sniffing glue; the plot follows one young addict whose sister convinces him of the danger that drugs pose.

In both films, the presence of workshop leaders at the screening is vital to deliver the message. After watching the film, the children are asked to comment on the characters' behaviour, prompted by questions such as, "What makes one person use drugs while others manage to avoid them?"

Among my various achievements, I am especially proud of my association with SKI, which continues today with the talented David Pell as its executive director. SKI's objectives have expanded to encompass subjects as controversial, in their own way, as AIDS was in the late 1980s. Today, the organization's activities include addressing the right of street kids to be employed. This issue produces resistance from some well-meaning people who object to the concept of children working, fearing their labour will be exploited by unfair employers paying subsistence wages.

SKI's stance is that yes, danger clearly exists, but children need to eat, and if being employed puts food in their stomachs and a roof over their heads, that is preferable to starving and freezing to death in the street. SKI teaches children to deal with the issue by acquiring skill sets and marketing them to their advantage. Its efforts have helped to create employment opportunities such as bicycle courier services in India and Sudan, a shoeshine collective in the Dominican Republic, a wholesale candy business in Peru, and a pizzeria in Tanzania. These may sound minuscule compared with the scope of the global problem, but efforts like these prove that progress can be made, and progress has a happy habit of multiplying itself. To assist its efforts in generating employment, SKI is launching a third animated film directed toward this goal and building on the past success of *Karate Kids* and *Goldtooth*.

I HAD NOT ACCOMPANIED Peter, Derek, and Kai on their consultations with street children while shaping *Karate Kids*, choosing to remain in Canada and keep travel costs to a minimum. The tales they told on their return, and the praise we received for our efforts to help street children, created an urge within me to stay connected in some way to these kids beyond my participation in SKI. I promised myself that I would remain committed to working on behalf of children in Third World countries, visiting the countries where street kids suffered daily, and experiencing their lives to the degree that I could. When the opportunity arose a few years later, I almost regretted keeping my promise.

I had met Foreign Affairs Minister Lloyd Axworthy at various political and social events, and when he invited me to join him on a trip to the African nation of Sierra Leone, I eagerly accepted. I wanted to sample first-hand the challenges facing children in Third World countries and perhaps find new ways of assisting them.

Sierra Leone is a country that, in a fair world, would be a paradise for its citizens, blessed as it is with both agricultural opportunities and large reserves of gem-quality diamonds. Instead of a paradise, I found hell on earth.

We arrived in 1999 while Sierra Leone was in the midst of an election. The Opposition leader, a madman named Foday Sankoh, was portraying himself as the Great Liberator of his country. Sankoh had learned his guerrilla tactics and ruthlessness from Libyan dictator Moammar Gadhafi, and for ten years after returning to Sierra Leone he and his followers waged a war against their own people, a war that in the scope of its cruelty and viciousness has been rarely surpassed in this day and age, even by the horrors of Rwanda and Uganda.

Sankoh headed a rebel army that had recruited many boys, some no older than ten or twelve. I met and spoke with one of them. A spindly kid with an AK-47 slung over his back, he had followed rebel orders to kill his parents before fleeing into the jungle, where he became one of Sankoh's revolutionaries. More than a grisly test of the boy's prowess and willingness to fight for Sankoh, killing his parents meant the boy was left with no family and no obligation other than to Sankoh. As a tactic for recruiting fighters, it was brilliant. As a measure of humanity, it was loathsome.

Lloyd Axworthy hoped to meet with Sankoh a[...] him to release the children from his organization, prepared to discuss and negotiate terms, if necessary. Neither of us was prepared for the unmitigated horror I witnessed.

The government party, seeking re-election, had chosen as its slogan *The Future Is in Your Hands*. Sankoh responded not with a slogan of his own but with callous terror. In an act of brutality that defies understanding, Sankoh's supporters began hacking off the hands of those suspected of backing the government. The future was in *their* hands, and Sankoh would remove both. I saw hundreds of citizens who were missing one hand, sometimes both. Many were children as young as three or four.

Sankoh and his people didn't stop at hands, nor did they stop at limbs. They hacked off feet, ears, and lips. They abducted young girls, hauling them to their camps, where they were repeatedly raped, and when the soldiers were finished with the girls, they either killed the girls or burnt out their eyes—*burnt out their eyes!*—and sent them back to their villages as examples of the rebels' powers. How is it possible that innocent children are treated like this, and how, as members of the human race, can Westerners pretend that this does not happen, that it does not concern us, that we are so different from these people that we need not become involved?

I never met Sankoh, who died while being held for trial shortly after I returned to Canada. I never had the opportunity to even attempt to understand how a man could order such things.

What drove the rebels of Sierra Leone to such levels of barbarity? It was not political or military goals. It was diamonds.

Sierra Leone diamonds represent a source of wealth in an otherwise impoverished country, and they are literally for the taking. The government controlled the mines, and whoever controlled the government had access to the cash that the mines generated. The idea that children would lose their limbs and young girls would suffer the agony of rape before having their eyes burned out, all motivated by the desire of wealthy Westerners to flash diamonds on their finger, around their neck, or in their earlobes, sickens me. (Recently, Hollywood became aware of the horrors of Sierra Leone and produced a movie, *Blood Diamond*, covering the events I described.) The images of maimed and blinded children gnaw at me still, and they fuel my incentive to make a difference in the world, especially where children are concerned.

TWELVE

A Goal Achieved
and a
Dinner Missed

In exchange for Nobby Gilmore's invaluable assistance to the film project, I had promised that I would lend Nobby a hand on behalf of the wider problem of AIDS, this one closer to home.

Nobby had mentioned that several people across the country were making efforts to tackle the AIDS crisis, with varying levels of success and credibility. Among them were Cornelia Molson, Jack Creed, Barry Campbell, Skippy Seymour, and others who had a reputation for being effective fundraisers. What we needed, Nobby suggested, was a national body composed of capable people who could be more effective than the various ad hoc groups, and he asked me to assist him in setting it up. This led to my co-founding the Canadian Foundation for AIDS Research, or CANFAR.

The goals of CANFAR were admirable, but it faced a practical problem back in the 1980s. The stigma AIDS carried meant a black-tie event that might have been an effective fundraiser for cancer or heart disease research simply wouldn't work for CANFAR. I had great fears of four or five embarrassed foundation members standing in an empty ballroom, creating an image of failure and rejection from which the group would never recover.

Fortunately, someone came up with a good idea. Instead of booking a hotel facility, we would make use of houses with snoop appeal—fabulous homes in Toronto's Rosedale and Forest Hill neighbourhoods. Ten or twelve invited guests would pay $500 each for a catered dinner, to be served in the exclusive residences of wealthy supporters. It couldn't fail, because we would recruit only as many homes as we needed for the tickets we sold. Things became even more promising when we discovered that the best caterers in the city would heavily discount their fees or even provide food gratis for the opportunity to connect with people who could afford $500 each for a charity event.

The results were wonderful. We raised a significant amount of money for the foundation in that first year alone, and maintained the program for several years. The foundation continues to this day, and I remain proud of my role in getting it started.

I am no longer a member of the CANFAR board. My decision to resign had nothing to do with either the board's activities or my own participation and everything to do with my philosophy of public service. I believe each period of contribution by me and other board members carries a best-before date. After making the maximum contribution in time and energy I can afford, I feel that it's time to take my sense of accomplishment home with me, and so encourage a new member with fresh ideas and energy to replace me. The best new board members bring new perspectives on old problems, and they feel free to question whether the old way of doing things is still the best way.

So much in the world could be accomplished if more people committed themselves to public service by joining boards where their values and talents are compatible with the organization's goals. That's something of a truism, I know, but I also believe that volunteer board members should not assume that their position is permanent. Charity boards need new ideas and new energy every bit as much as corporate boards. Perhaps more. Good people should move along, looking for new challenges and new places to use their talents.

My canfar experience led me to something else entirely unexpected. Of all the causes I have supported, none has exceeded in scope the global movement to remove and banish landmines. These devices are more than demonic in nature. They are cruel and unfair manifestations of our failure to live in peace, and they represent the refusal of nations to accept responsibility for their actions.

Armies set landmines for military purposes and then abandon them to wreak destruction on innocent civilians. Few weapons are more horrendous in their impact. A mine capable of maiming or murdering an entire family may cost as little as $3 to produce, yet the price to locate, remove, and disarm that same weapon may reach $1000. To clear one hectare, it could cost more than $100,000. Civilians, often the poor and destitute, are expected to pay the higher cost either in cash or in lost limbs and lives. An estimated seventy million landmines remain buried in about a third of the world's countries, awaiting a person or animal to step on them. Want more statistics? They are astonishing.

Landmines kill or maim almost twenty thousand civilians each year, or more than one every thirty minutes every day. About one of every three mine victims is a child. Many mines are blasting limbs from children fifty years after the weapons were buried, decades past the point where the reason for the war can even be remembered.

The killing and maiming are appalling in themselves, but the ripple effects are just as grim. Providing medical care and prosthetic limbs for landmine victims diverts money from countries that desperately need those funds for social services. Added to that cost, victims of landmines become an economic burden in countries such as Afghanistan, Cambodia, Mozambique, Angola, Bosnia-Herzegovina, and others either near collapse or struggling to get back on their feet. And land that is not fully clear of mines remains useless for agriculture, schools, recreation, transportation, and other purposes. These reasons alone should be enough to initiate a global campaign in every country to eradicate landmines.

As often seems to happen in my life, past connections were behind yet another nudge, one that led me to my involvement in the anti-landmine campaign.

During the 1990 campaign that elected Jean Chrétien leader of the Liberal Party, I had made an effort to raise money in support of Minister of Foreign Affairs Lloyd Axworthy's bid for the post. To me, Lloyd was a politician who adhered to a strong system of values, a man willing to tackle many of the more pressing issues of our time. Unfortunately, it soon became clear that Chrétien had a lock on the race. With limited sources of funding, I was among those who suggested that Lloyd abandon his plans.

One day in 1998, I took a telephone call in my office at Proshred from a member of the Ministry of Foreign Affairs staff, who invited my wife, Nancy, and me to attend a celebration in Winnipeg honouring Lloyd's twenty years of community service. We had friends in Winnipeg whom we hadn't seen for some time, so we decided to make a weekend of it.

When Lloyd and I chatted in Winnipeg, he noted my experience in launching start-ups and asked if Nancy and I could meet him some day in Ottawa for lunch. We agreed, and over that lunch with Lloyd and his wife, we were introduced not only to the scope and human misery of the landmine situation but to Lloyd's convincing observation that it was important for civil society to become engaged in this issue. Then he made his pitch: Would I consider creating a foundation to address the issues among Canadians and to serve as a fundraising platform?

It is impossible not to be touched by the image of a child whose legs have been blown off by an anti-personnel landmine installed as part of a conflict totally unrelated to the young victim or his or her parents.

Shaken by what Lloyd had told me, I looked into the issue more deeply. It was compelling, and within a short time, I was busy recruiting volunteers to establish the Canadian Landmine Foundation. I was soon contacted by Mary McDonald, a former consultant on foreign affairs and a member of Axworthy's staff, who had been doing many of the same things. We agreed to join forces, with me acting as chair, recruiting members to serve on the board and with Mary serving as a very capable CEO.

When I agreed to support the anti-landmine movement in Canada, my heart was obviously with the poor rural dwellers in

Third World countries. Looking for contributions, I aimed my attention at the upper strata of society because, as Willie Sutton replied when somebody asked him why he robbed banks, "That's where the money is."

Recalling the CANFAR dinner concept, I suggested we sell tickets for $25,000 to contributors who would enjoy a sumptuous dinner at 24 Sussex Drive. What house in Canada, after all, holds more snoop appeal than the prime minister's residence? I was, of course, naive because 24 Sussex proved unsuitable for a number of reasons, including the limited number of guests it could accommodate. More to the point, it is against policy to use the prime minister's residence for a fundraising event. Rideau Hall would be ideal, but the governor general's residence was also out of bounds for a fundraising event. There was nothing, however, to prevent Her Excellency from agreeing to honour a list of selected guests in recognition of their contribution to a cause as worthy as the Landmine Foundation. Governor General Clarkson agreed. If the foundation submitted a list of guests, she would make Rideau Hall available as the site for a dinner in their honour.

Rideau Hall is a wonderful place, and many Canadians would love to sample a dinner there. But it does not carry the cachet of 24 Sussex Drive, which, after all, functions as the prime minister's private residence. It can also accommodate many more people for an event like the one we were planning. We determined that a select guest list would be assembled to honour those who had made significant personal contributions to the foundation. Others were recognized for efforts that went beyond monetary assistance.

The governor general's husband, John Ralston Saul, added to the event's impact by agreeing to join the Landmine Foundation board as patron. His presence, I suspect, helped ensure the evening's outstanding success. The guest list at that first Rideau Hall evening was impressive. Canadians from all walks of life attended, along with internationally renowned figures such as financier George Soros, U.S. senator Patrick Leahy, and Queen Noor of Jordan, who had assumed the mantle of leadership for the international organization following the death of Diana, Princess of Wales.

Queen Noor's attendance caused some agitation when, just days before the event, her secretary called to check the arrangements made for the private jet that would transport Queen Noor and her thirteen-person entourage from Washington to Ottawa. Private jet? What private jet? We had anticipated providing a first-class flight on Air Canada, being unaware that Queen Noor never flies on commercial airplanes for safety and comfort reasons. Thanks to the generosity of Galen Weston, who volunteered the use of his airplane, we were able to transport the queen and eleven of her staff to and from the dinner. The remaining two members had to travel by commercial flight. It was all worth it; the queen added lustre to the evening, which proved a great success.

In 1999, I was flying to New York with Dan Livermore, Canada's foreign affairs ambassador for landmines, at the invitation of the UN to discuss the situation. I planned to present the familiar (to most of my audience) statistics of pain, suffering, and death, emphasizing that we should not lose sight of the need to end the carnage. During my conversation with Dan, I mentioned how the method used to raise money for CANFAR, catered dinners in luxurious private residences, had inspired the success at Rideau Hall. Perhaps, I ventured, we could find a way to remove the elitist aspect and still make it work. Maybe we could even extend it beyond Canada to involve people in New York City, Florida, or wherever sufficient numbers of Canadians could be found. "Let's have friends and neighbours invite their friends and neighbours into their homes for dinner, just like any other Friday night," I suggested. "The difference would be that the hosts and guests would discuss the landmine problem and each would write a cheque, large or small." Then I added, "Wouldn't it be great if we had a thousand dinners on the same evening?"

At breakfast the next morning, Dan told me he was intrigued by the idea. "If we could find funding for you," he asked, "do you think you could organize a thousand dinners to raise funds for the project this year?"

"Absolutely," I replied without hesitation, and an hour later I stood in front of the UN and announced the program I called The Night of a Thousand Dinners—one night in the year when people who shared their concern over landmines could assist the movement by hosting a dinner, discussing the landmine issue, and asking their guests to make a donation to be used in rehabilitating landmine victims and clearing the devices.

The idea was received with great enthusiasm. When I finished, Ambassador Bill Luers, the U.S. representative, broke into a wide grin, threw his arm over my shoulder, and said, "I'm with you!" Now I had to make it work.

We didn't achieve a thousand dinners in the program's inaugural year, but in the first year, over thirty thousand people had registered to attend functions in twenty-nine countries around the world, each pledging monetary and moral support to the cause. Many guests and participants were ambassadors and government officials. In fact, a substantial number of Canada's diplomatic corps actively promoted the concept, supportive of the goal to banish landmines and intensely proud of Canada's leadership. These initial supporters weren't the common folk we expected to spearhead the idea. U.S. secretary of state Madeleine Albright held a dinner at the State Department in the program's first year, and her successor Colin Powell repeated her support by hosting a dinner the following year. When notable celebrities like Paul and Heather McCartney got behind the Night of a Thousand Dinners—the name reduced in these computer-dominated times to N1KD—international momentum really built up. Unfortunately, that's also when it began to stumble in Canada, the movement's birthplace.

Ottawa had been the site of negotiations for a treaty to ban anti-personnel landmines in late 1997. Known as the Ottawa Treaty and officially titled "The Convention on the Prohibition of the Use, Stockpiling, Production and Transfer of Anti-Personnel Mines and on Their Destruction," the treaty is a comprehensive international instrument for ridding the world of the scourge of mines, and deals with everything from mine production and trade to victim assistance, mine clearance, and stockpile destruction.

More than 120 governments eventually signed the treaty, which became binding under international law in March 1999, meaning it moved through the process faster than any treaty of its kind in history. Today, the treaty remains open for ratification by signatories and for accession by those countries that did not sign before March 1999.

As both a major instigator of the treaty and the site of its official signing, Canada could have solidified its role as a leader in this movement, but it has not. Canada lagged in supporting the landmine ban and, in my opinion, thanks to certain complexities in our federal system, has squandered an opportunity to be identified with one of the great moral movements of our time.

The commitment that Nancy and I made to the anti-landmine movement extended beyond moral and monetary support. We moved our home from Toronto to Ottawa primarily to work with and assist the Canadian Landmine Foundation. Our presence in Ottawa, we believed, would make us more effective in holding the politicians' feet to the fire and ensure they backed up their words with positive action. We hosted dinners in our home for members of both the House and the Senate, each event dedicated to building support for the landmine cause. We kept the decision makers informed and constantly aware of the global need to deal with the issue. With that much dedication to the cause, you can only imagine how disappointed we were when Canada abandoned its leadership role.

Essentially, it boiled down to this: The Ministry of Foreign Affairs controls ideas and initiatives, but the Canadian International Development Agency (CIDA) controls the money. It seemed to me that the people at CIDA were not sufficiently committed to supporting the Landmine Foundation. With their own agenda to pursue, they appeared to see the landmine campaign as little more than an unnecessary distraction.

After some time, when it became evident that CIDA was stonewalling, I made an end run around them and sought help directly from the Prime Minister's Office. "Look," I said at a meeting with the representatives of the PMO, "I had commitments made to me when I took on this project and, in my view, CIDA is not living up to them. What can we do about it?"

My complaint earned me a meeting with CIDA president Len Good. CIDA would live up to its commitment, Good informed me, but the funding would not come out of CIDA's operational budget; it would be money from the ministry's discretionary spending fund.

This amounted to something of a pyrrhic victory. True, we had that year's funding in hand, but the message was clear to me: This was a one-time event, and we should not come back to CIDA for future funding.

The United States quickly assumed the leadership role Canada abdicated. This is both distressing and ironic, because the U.S. State Department, of all people, remains committed to the program even though that country has not signed the Ottawa Treaty. In fact, the United States has contributed more money for the removal of landmines than any other country. I received clear indications that the U.S. State Department would have been delighted had Canada continued to play a leading role in the movement. We failed to do so because, through lack of funding, the Canadian Landmine Foundation shrank to a shadow of its former self.

Contributing to the collapse of Canadian support was Lloyd Axworthy's departure from federal politics. With Lloyd gone, the air went out of our balloon. His successor, John Manley, supported the foundation's goals, but no one is more passionate about a movement than the person who spurs it, and Axworthy was the spur that had been driving the process forward. John Manley soon assessed the landmine issue as a goal worth pursuing. Then, just as we were raising his awareness about the issue, he was replaced in his post by Bill Graham. Once again, we had to compete with other issues and concerns for the minister's time. By this time, the federal bureaucracy had turned against the idea, choosing to support other projects, becoming almost hostile to the landmine foundation. With neither champion nor funding, the foundation was clearly doomed.

Today, the foundation is known as Adopt-A-Minefield. The United States continues to be the largest funder.

Canada once occupied the high ground on one of the great humanitarian issues of our day, but we frittered it away thanks to petty infighting within our bureaucracy—something which is, unfortunately, endemic in the Canadian government. The penchant of Canada's federal bureaucrats to introduce unwarranted complexities and apply unnecessary inertia to any new idea is pronounced because they appear frightened of making any decision of any import on any subject. Our bureaucrats do not sit across the table, listen to your proposal, and say, "Sorry, this will not work for these reasons." Instead, they nod sagely, letting you believe you are making your point and that they are moving toward a decision. Later, you discover nothing has happened. Later still, you discover that nothing *will* happen.

In some instances, the attitude of this country's entrenched bureaucracy could be considered malicious against any group or person it arbitrarily selects. That's a harsh assessment, but it's based on personal experience.

December 5, 2002, marked the fifth anniversary of the signing of the Ottawa Treaty, and I dedicated a substantial amount of time that year to staging an event that would celebrate the signing of the treaty, linking Canada's pivotal role in its creation. To generate broad media coverage would require a state dinner, followed by an evening at Ottawa's National Arts Centre featuring entertainers from across Canada and around the world. The attendance of UN Secretary-General Kofi Annan would be essential.

When everyone I consulted agreed the anniversary was a terrific opportunity to further the cause, I began coordinating all the elements needed. One of the most pleasurable activities was contacting leading entertainers, including Paul McCartney, who assured me they were interested in attending and performing in Ottawa if the secretary-general were present.

The coordination needed to stage such an event is enormous, and I found myself living and breathing the planning twenty-four hours a day for several weeks. We needed to confirm available dates for various venues, and verify that the UN secretary-general would be available for those dates. Protocol demanded that we work upward from a third-level secretary through various stages to the secretary-general himself, keeping the lines open to all the other participants. The coordination was almost maddeningly complex but absolutely essential before any formal announcement could be made. It's a basic rule of international diplomacy and protocol: When dealing with world leaders, invitations are issued only after the invitee agrees to attend. No one is invited if the answer even risks being negative, in this way avoiding embarrassment on either side. The confirmation of attendance is a formality.

When the Privy Council told me that it would be issuing a formal invitation for the UN secretary-general to attend the celebration, I was elated. All my hard work, and the work of many volunteers, to confirm venue dates, line up sponsors, launch security plans, arrange for transportation and meals, and perform a dozen other duties, was about to pay off. Everything, of course, was dependent on the attendance of Kofi Annan, but since the Privy Council had confirmed that his formal invitation had been sent, I had no reason to doubt his presence.

A few days later, I attended an event in New York. Secretary-General Kofi Annan was in attendance, and I approached him, introduced myself, identified my association with the Landmine Foundation, and said, "I understand you will be visiting us in Ottawa to celebrate the fifth signing of the landmine treaty."

The secretary-general looked confused, then sad. "I'm afraid I will not," he said. "I told your prime minister two weeks ago that I am not coming."

Two weeks ago? For two weeks, bureaucrats at the Prime Minister's Office and elsewhere in the government had known that the secretary-general would not be attending, yet no one informed me or anyone else working to make the event an international success. How could this be? Since the attendance of someone as highly placed as Secretary-General Kofi Annan is always confirmed *before* the invitation is issued, he had to have changed his mind. What had motivated him to cancel, and why had it been kept quiet?

Surely the change of heart had nothing to do with the secretary-general's backing for the landmine treaty; he supported its objectives then, and he has supported them since. So what were his reasons for cancelling? Apparently, they were related to the imminent invasion of Iraq by the United States, and that country's growing disdain for the UN. Things were made more complex by Prime Minister Jean Chrétien's refusal to commit

Canadian troops to the Iraq conflict, making Ottawa a less-than-favoured destination for the secretary-general in the eyes of Washington. In that atmosphere, the secretary-general felt it prudent to reject the invitation.

I felt I had acquired a sharp insight into the twists and turns of dealing with Canada's federal bureaucracy, but the incident with Secretary-General Kofi Annan proved I had underestimated it. Beyond my own humiliation, there is a lesson worth sharing, because I believe it explains so many frustrating aspects of this country.

The actions of Ottawa's mandarins would never be tolerated in the business world, where a deal is considered a deal. Break your word or contract in the real world—the world that lies beyond the boundaries of the National Capital Region—and you'll find yourself in court, trying to explain your actions to the judge. The problem lies in the fundamental difference between business and politics. Successful businesspeople work toward goals that are often several years in the future. Politicians must adhere to a shorter-term view, one that may not extend past the next election. That's the *reason* for breaking deals. But it should not be an excuse.

The average citizen may complain about the absence of a code of ethics among businesses, an observation that is neither as correct nor as widespread as many assume. Having been an active participant in both the business and government arenas, I have found that the business world is the more equitable of the two. Every degree of respect and trust that is lost in your business dealings is one more limit on your chances of future success. In contrast, the interpretation of ethics at the federal level is subject to the whims of the Prime Minister's Office, and it reflects the political realities of the day. As a result, what's promised today may be withdrawn tomorrow, and neither explanation nor consolation will be offered.

I had never been so personally affected by this attitude before the incident with Kofi Annan, and the impact rocked me. It also caused me to reflect on other aspects of the bureaucratic mindset that I had encountered. This is one of the finest countries in the world, and I am fully aware that our political decisions and actions are at least partially responsible for that position. It's the prevailing bureaucratic attitude that disturbs me, to the point where I continue to decline offers to seek a seat in Parliament, even though I believe (unlike a number of cynics) that politics is indeed an honourable profession. As a citizen dedicated to various issues, both social and economic, I would feel privileged to sit in the House of Commons. But as a bruised veteran of government's changing whims, I'm afraid it would be a torturous experience.

My association with Street Kids International (SKI) continues to be a source of great pride to me. SKI has been internationally recognized for the quality of its work and for the positive impact it has made for many of the most destitute citizens in this world—the hundred million homeless children, on every continent. No one doubts the effectiveness of SKI or the brilliance of its former executive director, Rosemary McCarney. For a few years, the federal government supported SKI by providing a portion of the organization's funding, recognizing the good work SKI performs on behalf of needy children around the globe.

Yet, in a knee-jerk reaction of political expediency, the federal government announced one day in 2004, without notice of any kind, that it was ending its funding immediately. When pressed for an explanation, the response was "budget restraints." Any organization dependent on federal government funding of any kind lives literally day to day, with the possibility of economic collapse arriving in the shape of a letter, a telephone call, or a phrase uttered on the floor of the House. This kind of crippling action is taken over and over again. Why do the politicians do it? Because they are permitted to.

Nancy and I have hosted countless dinners in our home for guests from both sides of the House, including cabinet ministers and a healthy representation of bureaucrats, all as part of our lobbying on behalf of the Landmine Foundation. The politicians, with one exception, expressed their enthusiastic support for the landmine treaty. Stephen Harper hesitated to, wondering if Canada's support might be frowned on by the Americans, non-signatories to the deal. But this was hardly a valid reason. The only objection to the agreement came from some bureaucrats at CIDA, who wanted no part of the program. It seemed to me that our elected representatives were taking a positive position on a subject of global interest and importance, yet they were constantly vexed by unelected career mandarins who sought to shape Canadian policy according to their own needs and perceptions.

This is no way to run a country. It indicates, among other things, that Canada has no vision and few core values, and that decisions can be made and promises broken with as much warning as a sudden change in the weather, and even less explanation.

I have dealt with government bureaucracy in both Canada and the United States, and the difference between the two could not be more dramatic. Most of my contact with the U.S. bureaucracy has been through that country's State Department, and in every deal in which I have been involved, the Americans lived up to their word. Whenever I made a presentation or submitted a proposal to U.S. government representatives, I received a clear response—either yes, this fits our parameters and we can work with you on the project, or no, we cannot support you on this one. You cannot have a meeting like that in Canada. While we have many fine individuals in this country's civil service corps, too often it appears that our bureaucrats will "take it under advisement." In the United States, you get the straight goods. In Canada, you get blank looks and a reaction to match. That's been my experience, and no one familiar with working on both sides of the border at that level has disagreed with me.

Here's another fact that disturbs this otherwise rabid Canadian nationalist: If U.S. government officials respond positively to your proposal or presentation, they will not stop there. They'll get creative, looking for ways to maximize the program's impact and effectiveness, often with unconditional responses like, "That's a pretty good idea—we'll fund it." I have found too often the Canadian response to be "We'll give you part of the funding if you come up with the rest" or "We'll give you 10 or 15 or 20 percent, take it or leave it." If a project is worthwhile to Americans, it's worth paying for. The United States has its critics, including me on a number of topics, but this aspect is one that other nations can emulate, and none more than Canada.

So why did the United States refuse to sign the landmine treaty? My understanding is that the U.S. government had agreed in principle to sign the treaty if it was granted an exemption in the case of the Korean demilitarized zone, the no man's land between North and South Korea. In 1997, on the eve of the treaty's signing, U.S. president Bill Clinton conferred with then prime minister Jean Chrétien in a late-night telephone call. If you can get us a five-year exemption on Korea, Clinton reportedly said to Chrétien, the United States will come on board. Chrétien agreed, but a number of non-governmental organizations disagreed; as far as they were concerned, it was an all-or-nothing deal. Their intransigence prevented the United States from adding its name to the agreement, a foolish move in my opinion.

That same year, the United States made an agreement with Slovenia concerning landmines in the Balkans. The Slovenians were assured by the Clinton government that if Slovenia set up a trust fund to pay for the cost of removing landmines in the region, soliciting funds from supporting nations, the United States would match and double that amount annually. Slovenia agreed and, every year since 1997, it has amassed millions of dollars to remove and disarm landmines, and every year the U.S. government has lived up to its end of the bargain. In addition, the United States has not laid one landmine since 1993. So even though that country is not a signatory to the agreement, it has been acting as though it were. Perhaps someone should alert Stephen Harper.

THE FAILURE OF MY PROPOSAL to celebrate the landmine treaty and the collapse of the event that was to feature UN Secretary-General Kofi Annan was the first of two major disappointments that year. The second arrived a few weeks later.

I received an invitation to attend an event in Washington hosted by then U.S. secretary of state Colin Powell, who had continued the tradition of his predecessor Madeleine Albright of being the first each year to host a Night of a Thousand

Dinners. I had attended the previous year's event and was looking forward to taking part again.

Travelling from Ottawa on the day of the dinner, I planned a stopover in Toronto on my way to Washington. Before leaving to catch the flight that morning, I mentioned to my wife, Nancy, that I wasn't feeling all that well—not badly enough to cancel the trip, just a little ill. Things got no better during the flight to Toronto. By the time we landed, a pain in my side had developed and was growing more severe. I had planned to meet Dianne Chabot, CEO of The Mount Pleasant Group, to discuss some business matters. Greeting her, I explained my discomfort and asked if she would mind walking with me to a nearby medical clinic, where I might get something to dull the nagging pain. We discussed business on the way, and when we reached the clinic, I bade her goodbye.

The clinic staff, unsure of the cause of my discomfort, suggested I visit nearby St. Michael's Hospital. On my way there, I called Nancy back in Ottawa from my cell phone and described my pain, but said that I was still planning to join the secretary of state for dinner in Washington. Nancy, her sharp instincts intact, suspected it was more than indigestion. She telephoned my sister-in-law, Michèle, asking her to check up on me at the hospital.

Emergency room doctors and nurses poked and probed at the site of the pain before rolling me in for an X-ray. One glance at the film identified the source of my rapidly increasing agony: a swollen appendix. An operation was scheduled for the next day. There went my dinner with Colin Powell. After passing on my regrets, I looked up to see Greig Clark, my old venture capital fund buddy, approaching. Just as we settled into a chat, the pain that I thought was merely severe elevated to volcanic proportions. My appendix had burst. As I tossed in agony from one side of the bed to the other, Michèle ran for assistance. The next day's scheduled operation was now only minutes away.

The operation was a success and, while I regretted missing the dinner with Colin Powell, the disappointment was softened the next day when I received a telephone call from Rideau Hall. It was John Ralston Saul, asking about my health and expressing wishes for a speedy recovery from him and Governor General Adrienne Clarkson. While this was gratifying to me, it was tremendously impressive to the hospital staff, and I sensed a subtle change in the attention I received from that point on.

THIRTEEN

A Village in the Snow

In many ways, my life has been a search for the core of my spirituality and its link to a Higher Power, however that term may be defined. I suspect I am not very different from most people in this sense. We all tread toward the same goal; only the paths we follow are dissimilar. The path I followed was at times frightening, but also interesting and enlightening.

I write this in a somewhat low spiritual mood. I am currently in a blue place, to use Father Bill's analogy of the stained-glass window. I fully expect to move toward a warmer orange or red place. It will happen later today, tomorrow, whenever.

During the years I lived in Toronto, I attended church on weekdays but never for Sunday Mass, because that's the day the Church *expected* me to be there. The services during the week were refreshing to me in many ways. Like most people of a religious persuasion or who possess a certain depth of spiritual belief, I drew comfort from the presence of others who were seeking the same things—solace, assurance, hope, or perhaps just the revival of warm memories.

While I love the experience of attending church, I have problems with the institution of the Catholic Church itself. I cannot abide its attitude toward women, dictating the limits of their role within the Church and the limits of their decision making when it comes to birth control and abortion. Such male dominance may reflect values at the time of Christ, but no one has shown me where Jesus preached that we were to change nothing from that period. I know of no sermons delivered by Christ in which he taught that we were to wear only robes, or reject the benefits of plumbing and the comfort of central heating. How can we adjust to these modern times and continue to treat women as though it were 30 A.D.?

Still, we take our daughters to Sunday Mass. I benefit from the ambience, and I enjoy the company and conversations of intelligent, empathetic priests, in spite of the abuse I suffered as a boy. Goodness and evil can surely abide in the same institution, and perhaps even in the same person.

LIKE OTHERS, I HAVE EXTENDED my spiritual quest beyond the bounds of the Church. In the years between leaving Second Cup and meeting Nancy, I attended regular meetings with people who had trod through expanses of wilderness similar to the one I had emerged from, managing to shed their substance abuse and self-destructive tendencies along the way. While we were thankful for our success and proud of our personal achievements, gratitude alone was not enough. We continued looking for something more. Even when we grew unsure of finding whatever we were searching for, it didn't matter. The quest was what counted, along with the companionship of others on the same mission.

I don't want to suggest that these sessions were some sort of Council of Trent or ecumenical debate, because they were not. We met to discuss our concerns and our discoveries, to evaluate our successes and our failures. Sometimes the sessions were serious and deep; sometimes they were social and gossipy. We were basically a bunch of people looking for a connection to a Higher Power, using our experience as the home base for the search. These meetings extended over several years and, as you can imagine, they addressed myriad topics from multiple points of view.

Did we experience any epiphanies, define any eternal truths, or elevate any viewpoints to the level of dogma and creed? No, no, and no. Yet, hardly anyone missed a session; the meetings were that important to us. To me, they were an essential way to stay in touch with my spirituality, and I continued to attend them as long as I lived in Toronto, even after Nancy and I married.

When I moved to Ottawa in 2000, the opportunity to engage in those discussions vanished, and my spirituality has suffered as a result. That's why I feel in a blue place. Things will change, I know. While I no longer share the unique environment of those Toronto sessions, I maintain and strengthen links available to me through people on the same quest—friends like Phil Fontaine, the former national chief of the Assembly of First Nations and a very spiritual man. I also look forward to discussions with a retired priest whose wisdom and experience I value. In many ways, we all remain in the wilderness. But the light is better, the path is easier to follow, and the company is reassuring.

If someone asked me if I was religious, I would reply that spirituality works for me but dogma does not. I cannot be more specific than that.

YOU CAN TAKE THE MAN AWAY from politics, but it's nearly impossible to take politics away from the man. The energy, the goals, the competition of elections, have excited me since that first campaign with my father back in 1958. Soon after Nancy, the girls, and I settled in Ottawa, a federal election was called, and I couldn't restrain myself from becoming involved.

Stockwell Day, the new leader of the Reform Party, had been stirring up a great deal of interest. Some observers were comparing his dynamic image to that of Pierre Trudeau's, when he first arrived on the scene back in 1968. I did not share that opinion, and I felt that many of the planks in the Reform Party's platform ran counter to the things I valued, and I believed most other Canadians failed to share them as well. So I chose to support a local Liberal candidate.

Since my riding was heavily bilingual and I am not, I headed to Ottawa South, an anglophone riding, where I got involved in John Manley's campaign. My motivation was not entirely altruistic as far as the election effort was concerned. As the new foreign affairs minister, Manley would be highly influential in addressing the issue of landmines, and I saw my campaign contribution as a step toward building a trusting relationship with him.

Unfortunately, Manley was travelling a good deal at the time, and throughout the election campaign I never laid eyes on him. Still, I was reasonably content to do the mundane but necessary tasks of working the telephones and checking voters' lists.

Several months later, I happened to be flying to Toronto. I boarded the airplane, only to discover that someone had taken my seat. Since the flight was not full, I suggested he remain where he was, and I took one of the empty seats.

The last passenger to board strolled down the aisle and sat next to me. It was John Manley, the guy whose campaign I had worked on for several weeks without meeting him. Now here we were shoulder to shoulder for the flight to Toronto. We launched into conversation, and I soon mentioned the landmine issue. John was supportive of our efforts. In fact, our conversation grew so animated that we remained seated, discussing aspects of the problem after most passengers had deplaned. I asked John for his support, and he promised to do what he could.

That flight cemented a relationship that endures to this day. I was able to return the favour of John's help in moving the landmine program back into the limelight by volunteering my services to his Liberal Party leadership campaign, when he sought to replace Jean Chrétien. As deputy finance chairman, I worked with Tom McDougal from the law firm of Perley-Robertson, Hill & McDougal. Tom, a brilliant lawyer, filled the position of finance chair, while my job was to tour the country, along with Senator Marie Poulin, meeting important donors and raising funds for John's campaign.

We succeeded, to a degree. The campaign raised more money for John Manley's campaign than Jean Chrétien spent on his entire leadership campaign ten years earlier. Still, substantially more money would be needed to launch a challenge against leadership contender Paul Martin, and we might have raised it. When reality set in, however, and we realized we could not succeed against the numbers already in the Martin camp, we folded our tents.

Many Canadians, I know, share my belief that John Manley would have made a great prime minister, and perhaps he will someday.

Through the campaign, I became friends with Senator Poulin and her husband Bernard. Marie continues to work toward her law degree, an accomplishment for anyone at any age, and even more so for an active senator. Adding to her already heavy workload, she has assumed the presidency of the Liberal Party of Canada. Bernard is a gifted portrait artist, and together they represent one of this country's most admired couples.

Some people would say my assigned seat being occupied on that flight to Toronto, which in turn enabled me to buttonhole the minister of foreign affairs for an entire hour, was the expression of a Higher Power's support. Who knows? The important thing is it happened, and I was able to create something positive out of happenstance.

LIFE CONTINUES TO TEACH ME LESSONS, and I hope it always will. Sometimes these lessons arrive in unusual places and with unexpected messages.

I still own and fly an airplane. On a practical level, this allows me to commute quickly between Ottawa and ARXX Walls and Foundations in Cobourg, Ontario, where I enjoy serving the firm's shareholders as CEO. Flying satisfies an emotional need as well, one that I cannot wholly define. The best way I can describe it is a blend of solitude and pride, united in a spiritual context. Winging through often-crowded air space, I simultaneously enjoy the freedom of flying and the security of being watched and guided by air traffic controllers. The disembodied voices belong to people I will never meet yet whom I depend on for my safety and well-being. If you spot a religious aspect to that last observation, I won't be surprised.

Flying, too, teaches lessons, and they are always lessons worth heeding. Once, several years ago, I was returning from a winter vacation, piloting my twin-engine airplane home from Nassau with three passengers aboard. We left late in the day, tracing the coastline north toward Toronto, and soon we were enveloped in darkness. Flying at night is often easier and more relaxing than during the day: The air tends to be stabilized, traffic in the sky is lighter, and on clear nights you can see for hundreds of kilometres, identifying large cities as landmarks. This trip began on a beautifully clear night, and things couldn't have been better for the first few hours.

As we were about to cross Lake Ontario, however, we encountered a huge winter storm, which was pelting Toronto with freezing rain. Landings at the airport were backed up, and for the first time in my flying life I was placed in a holding pattern, circling in the sky awaiting my turn to land. Anxiety over ice building up on the wings, always a concern to pilots in winter, made me a little nervous, especially when the air traffic controller told me I should expect to hold for about forty-five minutes.

So I was relieved when, shortly after I entered the holding pattern, the controller informed me of an opening and that I could begin my approach immediately. "But keep your speed up," he added. "There's a 747 in line to land behind you." The controller gave me the position for my landing approach. I followed his instructions and focused on getting the airplane and my passengers back on the ground safely.

I failed to pick up the clue that something was wrong when the controller asked about my speed. I replied that it was 180 knots, much higher than it should have been. I was concerned that he wanted even more speed from me. After all, he had warned me to stay well ahead of the 747.

When I broke out of the clouds and saw the airport below, I realized that I was well to the left of the runway and so began correcting my position. Once I was centred, I reduced the speed, felt the airplane begin to descend, silently congratulated myself on my expertise, and cut the power to the engines. With that move, every alarm on the control panel went off—lights flashed, bells rang, and buzzers sounded, all warning me that I had neglected to lower the landing gear! I hit the lever, the wheels came down and locked just as we touched the ground, and we held on while the airplane rolled down the runway at a very high speed. To make things even scarier, the runway was ice-covered, so I dared not use my brakes. It took the entire length of the runway to stop, a distance of about 10,000 feet or roughly two miles.

Later, I understood the controller's question about the airplane's speed. He could read it on his radar scope, and he suspected that my airplane could not maintain that speed with the landing gear down. Air traffic controllers are trained not to question a pilot's decision except in clearly dire circumstances. In this case, he questioned my unusual speed and it was up to me to

216

review my actions. Pilots accept this arrangement. My airplane, for example, could have been modified to handle a faster landing speed with the gear lowered, something he could not have known. I had missed interpreting his concern, with almost disastrous results. The lesson? Never take anything for granted. Don't focus on one aspect of life at the expense of others. Or perhaps: Always listen carefully to the words of someone you depend on.

I REMAIN AS PROUD of the direction my life has taken since that cold day on Jarvis Street as you might expect. Yet that guy in the filthy T-shirt who stumbled up the stairs seeking help is still, in more ways than anyone could guess, the same man who walked up the red carpet at Rideau Hall on May 14, 2004, to be declared an Officer of the Order of Canada by Governor General Adrienne Clarkson. I stood thinking of him as the declaration awarding me this exceptional honour was read:

> Frank O'Dea's triumph over adversity continues to captivate the hearts of Canadians. His personal victory over substance abuse and willingness to share his rags-to-riches story have inspired others battling addiction. He enjoyed enormous success as co-founder of the Second Cup chain of coffee shops and has gone on to other business ventures. His many good works include support of Street Kids International, which is devoted to protecting homeless children around the world from predators. Founding chair of the Canadian Landmine Foundation, he created and launched the Night of a Thousand Dinners annual fundraising event that has raised over $2 million for their cause.

He had come a long, long way from Jarvis and Shuter.

As part of the ceremony, I was asked to identify the person whom I most admired and who influenced me the most. After spinning the Rolodex in my mind, I replied: "My father."

I had come to realize that the teenager who lied and stole to get alcohol had been the antithesis of everything my father had taught me about values and behaviour. By example, if not by discussion, Dad had imbued in me a powerful sense of honesty and self-sufficiency, along with an obligation to serve your community to the best of your ability. Through all those years spent in an alcoholic haze, I was betraying the best lesson parents can deliver to their children, one that my father, as inarticulate and passive as he might have seemed to me, wanted me to absorb. From the perspective of thirty-five years later, I can see that this realization came percolating down to me when I stood in the park on that cold December morning. I had betrayed the lessons Dad attempted to instil in me, and I did it in ways that must have agonized him. I now believe that was the power that motivated me to walk away from skid row and up the stairs to the woman who smiled at the sight of me and said, "You're home."

I wished beyond description that my father and mother were still alive and able to watch me receive that honour in Rideau Hall. On the other hand, I was delighted that my wife, my children, and my brother Sean were there to be part of it. Sometimes we must rejoice in embracing aspects of our lives that are both valued and available, and mourn the absence of others. I will always be aware, however, that a vital part was missing from that experience.

In June 2005, I received another honour that measured the distance I had travelled. Royal Roads University granted me an honorary Doctor of Laws degree. As proud as I was to receive this recognition, I took equal pride in the opportunity to address that year's graduating class. I faced several hundred students eager to tackle the world with their newly acquired knowledge. After several years of study and preparation (and substantial student loans for many, I suspect), they were understandably anxious to exchange their skills and education for an income. I understood that, but I asked them to always remember some wisdom I had gained over my life's journey to that point. "It's not the money you make that matters most," I said. "It's the difference you make." The standing ovation I received confirmed that my message got through to them and made an impact.

Of course, some things resist change, no matter how far the journey or how extended the time. Receiving my honorary degree and addressing the students created as much pride and sense of accomplishment in me as you might expect. But not totally. A small part of me was still the kid who had been sexually exploited, the teenager who had wrecked cars and endangered the lives of others, and the young man who stood shivering in the rain, his hand extended and his hopes never reaching beyond the next coin in his hand, the next swallow of wine, the next evening of oblivion. This aging, distant part of me whispered to me from time to time, "You are a fraud." I take some consolation in the knowledge that others like me, who have turned back their demons, share the same experience.

Along with my faith and my marriage, I find comfort in a poem by Max Ehrmann that was popular among young people when I was a Jarvis Street fixture. Titled "Desiderata," its words became something of a prayer for that generation. You will no doubt recognize the opening lines:

Go placidly amid the noise and haste,
and remember what peace there may be in silence.
As far as possible without surrender
be on good terms with all persons.

The last lines, familiar to you I'm sure, resonate within me when I recall those early years and all the pain and confusion I experienced:

You are a child of the universe
no less than the trees and the stars;
you have a right to be here.
And whether or not it is clear to you,
no doubt the universe is unfolding as it should.

Therefore be at peace with God,
whatever you conceive Him to be,
and whatever your labors and aspirations,
in the noisy confusion of life,
keep peace with your soul.

With all its sham, drudgery, and broken dreams,
it is still a beautiful world.
Be cheerful. Strive to be happy.

THIS WOULD BE A GOOD place to end my story. But I have one more tale.

While I named my father as the greatest influence in my life when receiving the Order of Canada, I chose not to mention some negative aspects to this influence. One of them was the distancing between him and his children, an attitude that I consciously reject. When Nancy and I became parents, I vowed that I would never be as distant from our girls as my father had been from his children.

When the girls were younger, I began a ritual of reading them a bedtime story each night, a custom that we—Taylor, Morgan, and I—maintain to this day. I read these stories from books until I heard someone on CBC Radio describing how he made up each night's bedtime story, beginning with the same setting and characters spinning different tales each night. I thought this was a wonderful idea and one evening, when it was time to tell my daughters their story, I set the book aside and began:

"There is a little village high in the mountains, where every day it snows. And in a corner of the village is a little house where a little old lady lives. Behind her house is a barn, and in the barn live a horse named George, a cow named Moo, and a bird named Tweet." Every story starts in this same way.

I have been spinning yarns for Taylor and Morgan for years now, and I can make the girls burst into laughter simply by saying, "There is a little village high in the mountains ..." while raising my hands over my head and flicking my fingertips to suggest falling snow.

I have surprised myself with my ability to create stories about the village and the little old lady and her barn animals. Sometimes my stories encompass others in that village where it snows every day, and in one way or another, the village has become real to us. If the girls were to close their eyes and picture the village, I'm sure they would see its inhabitants, who will always be safe and happy. There will be a friendly cop on the corner, a cute church in the centre of town, a dog wagging its tail in the park, children playing and laughing, and adults greeting each other with smiles and warm wishes.

But there will not be any people living on the street and begging for money to buy a drink.

Not a one.

ACKNOWLEDGMENTS

A great many people made this story possible. I'm thinking particularly of great friends I have made on my journey such as Bill and Joanna Orr, Clint and Norma Jean Calder, Ron and Judy Bannerman, Peter Haight, Peter Armstrong, Gerry Pesket, and Peter Watters, among others. These folks epitomize hope in all its forms.

To the people at Penguin Books Canada, editorial director Diane Turbide and production editor Sandra Tooze, and also to my copy editor, Judy Phillips, I quote René Lévesque: "I sincerely hope that my publishers will not regret the risks that they were taking—not to mention my own—by throwing me into such an adventure." I am grateful for your patience and persistence.

Thanks also to my agent, Hilary McMahon, for her focus and dedication to making this book, which became the best possible catharsis.

And finally, thanks are due to John Lawrence Reynolds, my writer, and Judy, John's wife, for her muffins. Hope, patience, and persistence are the hallmark of John's writing. He is more than a writer; he has become a friend. John was able to capture my feelings and communicate in such a beautiful way that which I was trying to say. Thanks, John.